The New Author

A beginner's guide on how to write a novel,
publish as an independent ebook author and
promote your brand using social networks

RUBY BARNES

Print Edition

Published by Marble City Publishing

Copyright 2012 by Ruby Barnes

All rights reserved

ISBN 10 1908943076

ISBN 13 978-1-908943-07-1

The scope of this book is deliberately limited to basic novel writing guidelines, first practical steps in building and operating a social media platform for authors, and the process of epublishing a novel on Amazon KDP and other market channels via Smashwords. A list of recommended further reading is provided that covers the subject matter, should readers wish to delve deeper into these areas.

This edition of The New Author does not contain a method approach to novel writing, advice on publishing in print or a prescriptive 'silver bullet' approach to ebook marketing.

The internet is a labyrinth of blogs, websites and web-based tools. User interfaces are constantly being improved, upgraded and changed. No screenshots have been included in this book in order to avoid early obsolescence and to keep the format and page display simple and readable.

Every effort has been made to ensure the accuracy of the content of this book, but the nature of publishing is continuously changing and internet platforms are constantly updated. The publisher and author assume no responsibility for errors, inaccuracies, omissions or inconsistencies contained within. They disclaim any personal liability, directly or indirectly, for advice or information presented. The book is sold with the understanding that neither the author nor publisher is engaged in rendering any legal, psychological or accounting advice.

.

Dedication

For Adrienne, John and Suzanne

Contents

Foreword

From Jim Williams, author of ten internationally published novels including the Booker Prize nominated *Scherzo*. His most recent novel is *The English Lady Murderers' Society*.

The New Author is an excellent piece of writing, combining deceptive simplicity, lucidity and charm: a trick which in practice is very difficult to pull off. The book is also informed by considerable intelligence and analysis founded on firsthand experience. Ruby Barnes has succeeded in e-publishing and he knows what he's talking about.

The book is simply and logically structured in three parts. The first part deals with what can loosely be called the Rules of Writing. This is not specific to the e-format and covers the commonly accepted points of writing technique in a clear commonsense manner and with an appropriate level of scepticism as to the possibility of writing by rule. It's a useful summary and most writers probably need nothing more. The truth is that the trick is in the practice not the theory, and what most aspiring writers need is informed critique of concrete pieces of work.

The heart of the book is in the second part, which is explains how to parlay your e-book into a bestseller by leveraging the opportunities provided by Twitter and social networking sites to create a product brand, and an aware and active readership.

For six hundred years the printed codex has been the technical format of books. The e-book looks set to displace that codex as the preferred reading format. I can envisage a future in which books develop almost as two separate art forms, like theatre and film. A small stratum of bestsellers may survive as hard format books, sold through limited outlets suited to casual readers, and behind this will be the cloud of e-books. Where does "choice" stand in this scenario? In the world of the hard format, it will be very reduced. In the realm of the e-book, however, the range of choice will be vast as new entrants, who in the past would have been excluded from being published through bad luck or incompetence, pile into e-books. Here the question is whether the enhanced choice will be meaningful, or perceived as white noise, a mere cacophony.

Ruby Barnes's book faces up to this changed scenario and says – rightly, I think – that predictable success can only happen through deliberate manipulation of social networking in all its forms. In the second part of The New Author he takes the reader in detail through various techniques for doing this and identifies key forums of opinion.

The third part is a detailed exposition of how to convert a manuscript into an e-publishable form compatible with commercial e-readers. It goes on to explain how to place the book with a free e-publisher such as Amazon, and various post-publishing matters such as reviews, pricing and tracking of sales.

Barnes explicitly warns against the trap that engagement at the required level can become obsessive and time consuming, and in a couple of nice vignettes he makes his point with wit and style. The

New Author is a terrific companion for independent e-publishing and I recommend it.

Jim Williams

My grateful thanks to Jim Williams for taking the time to read *The New Author* and writing the above foreword.

There are at least three reasons why you should read this book:

1. you want to be an author;

2. you have already written a novel and want to publish it as an ebook;

3. you want to promote yourself as an author.

This book is a beginner's guide on how to do the above. It isn't a magic elixir for foolproof million copy marketing of your ebook. It is based upon the experiences of this author and a broad-based peer group.

I have to warn you right now, this is not going to be an easy journey. Less of a country stroll, more of a trek up Kilimanjaro. The good news is that almost anyone can trek up Kilimanjaro with the right support, appropriate equipment and a positive attitude. See you at the top.

RUBY BARNES

About the author

If you're worried I'm going to drag you off to my writing lair, show you my first pencil perfectly preserved in its hermetically sealed glass case, invite myself to dinner at yours, and then indoctrinate you into my personality cult, then please feel free to skip forward to the practical content of this book. Alternatively, if you want to know a little about me and why I wrote The New Author, then read on.

First things first, cards on the table and various other clichés. I'm not a million-selling author. This is the story of a regular guy who has learnt how to write, publish and market ebooks. I have a thirty year career behind me in international technology sales and work daytime in performance improvement. Marketing, strategy and influence are the way I think. Six years ago I decided to take my writing hobby to the next stage and write a novel. The day job had taken me to twenty-nine countries. I'd done business, got drunk and partied in most of them, so I figured that qualified me to write an international adventure novel à la Tom Clancy. I wrote that novel in six months, then I wrote another one, then I crashed down to earth with a bang. Agents and publishers weren't interested in my novels.

I paid good money to have my novel professionally assessed and it repeated what my long-suffering wife and beta-reader had been saying for the first year. Good plot, amateurish writing. She took me aside, by the ear, and thrust a newspaper advertisement in my face. National University of Ireland Maynooth -

Creative Writing for Publication. Three years later and the true horror of my early novels became apparent to me. Those works languish under my bed and that's the best place for them.

With the subsequent support of two multi-published authors as mentors, writer peer review groups in Kilkenny and Dublin, and two online review websites, I produced a third novel and then a fourth. I read and reviewed hundreds of novel excerpts, learning craft from the successes and mistakes of others, attempting to implement that learning in my own writing.

The third novel was quirky and genre-bending. Not quite a thriller, partly farce, dark humour, not literary, almost lad-lit. Agents and publishers began to reject it in droves. I figured it was part of the learning curve. My writing wasn't good enough, the concept insufficiently commercial, characters too unlikable etc. So I sucked it up and went ahead with the fourth novel, trying to keep one eye on commercial viability.

Then I had an epiphany. If the third novel wasn't going to get a breakthrough with traditional publishing then why not launch it as a Kindle ebook on Amazon? Nothing to lose. Here in Ireland folk just didn't understand. Ebooks? They'll never catch on. But the internet was humming with a global impetus that spoke of the future. Not being one for half measures I threw myself in at the deep end.

My college lecturer was fascinated by the brave new world of indie ebooks and asked me to write a paper on ebook publishing for the next year's students. I was happy to oblige and also embarked upon a series of blog posts covering various aspects of the authoring process. That was the springboard for my blog which subsequently had thousands of hits from writers and readers around the globe.

Modest success is how I would describe my first year as an independent ebook author. At the time of writing I have sales of just under twenty thousand ebooks, albeit many of those given free to obtain a readership. My blog has had over twenty thousand views, admittedly some of those looking for elephants rather than ebooks (more about SEO, tags and keywords later). I'm pretty sure that the twenty thousand common number of sales and blog views is coincidental. I've sent two thousand five hundred tweets to two thousand five hundred twitter followers, published seventy blog posts and accumulated six hundred plus friends on facebook. The mass of my social media platform continues to mushroom. My first novel occupies the first ten pages of title + author internet searches.

Am I still writing? Yes. I published a second novel in November 2011 and have the next one underway. Oh, and I wrote The New Author.

Mistakes have been made en route, some of them serious. I haven't had extraordinary luck and my brand was completely unknown before March 2011. I haven't sold a million ebooks but I have tens of thousands of readers and a brand that is en route to firm establishment. The way I look at it, if I can do it then anyone can.

RUBY BARNES

Part 1 - Writing a novel

This is not a comprehensive guide to novel writing. It's an overview of the different aspects of novel writing that a new author should consider. If you prefer a prescribed approach there are numerous extensive texts available containing detailed advice (see Recommended Reading at the end of this book).

Have you got what it takes?

I've always felt that I have a novel inside of me. When I hear someone say this, a mental image appears of surgery being performed on the speaker to extract their story. Dripping with the experience of life, it emerges from the donor, be it memoir, fiction or a travelogue of sub-Saharan Africa.

There is almost no one on this planet who has led a totally uninteresting life. Even then the reason that they have led such a life might in itself be interesting. A twenty-first century glut of celebrity memoirs and novels shows that everyone is capable of producing a story of sorts. The trick is in the writing. Does it engage the target audience? Fact or fiction, there is an art to storytelling. In Ireland a Shanachie is a gifted verbal storyteller. To hear one is to never forget the story or the Shanachie (Niall de Burca is a good example). A novel author should look to leave the same impression.

Unless you are trained in writing, it's unlikely that you will produce a best-selling masterpiece with your first attempt at writing a novel. Those that do often have an education and career in journalism behind them, having written to the moon and back.

Disheartened? Well, there is another alternative. Pick up one, or why not several, of the renowned How To books on writing. Read them all, digest and internalise the content and apply immediately to your writing. Wait a minute, isn't that writing by numbers? Will the result resemble a picture painted by numbers, similarly lacking in spontaneity and creativity? More than likely, yes.

So now we come to the crux of the matter. As a new author if you want to write a good novel then, in almost all cases, you need to build your experience of writing. You might be a marathon writer, throwing yourself at an entire novel. Alternatively you're a sprinter and that means short stories. Either way, a literary athlete. I hope you're dressed appropriately.

The time, space, support continuum

Now that you've made the decision to write (if you were already writing regularly then this doesn't apply), when, where and how are you going to do it? Here are some characteristic approaches.

The Hemingway - tortured author, tapping away on a typewriter in a mountain retreat. Wild hair, scant meals, sleep-deprived, continuously slightly drunk and chain-smoking.

The Media Junkie – listening to fast music on iPod or laptop, oblivious of the surroundings which might be a café, train, family TV room or workplace. Laptop has ten windows open for 'research' including email, twitter, facebook and Wikipedia.

The Midnight Oil – when the house is quiet and everyone else's day is over, this one is just starting work. Typing through the tiredness and pain barrier. Pulling together the inspiration of observations and events from the preceding daylight hours. Pausing to reflect upon the words written, listening to the drip of the bathroom tap, the hum of a transformer in some electrical apparatus somewhere in the house.

The Peacemaker – a scented candle, Buddha Bar on the music system. Pilates exercises performed with control and precision, establishing the inner core. Elsewhere in the house family rampage at a safe distance, out of earshot. Writing flows from the spirit. Characters talk aloud and their dialogue falls upon the keyboard.

The Early Bird – rising at the hour of milkmen from yesteryear, moving from bedroom to study and pushing the door firmly shut. Chapters formulated subconsciously during sleep are thrown onto the page to be edited during some lull in the day. As the family stirs, heading off to the bathroom and using time under the shower to think a way out of the present predicament of the main character.

What do you think of these approaches? I've tried them all at different times over the years. Any consistent method can be productive providing you ring-fence the time and space. That needs support and understanding from the other people in your life.

They need to understand and appreciate your needs as a writer.

The Rules

There are books about the rules of writing. If we all followed these rules to the letter then every novel would be the same – minimalist, adverb-free, grammatically perfect, sanitised, identical. You could probably write a computer programme and whack everyone's manuscript through it. House style.

In fact, the rules are just guidelines. It's fine to transgress them, as long as the result remains readable and entertaining. But that's like comedic bad piano playing. In order to hit a deliberate bum note, without derailing the whole piece, the pianist needs to be highly skilled.

Bestseller lists and award shortlists abound with examples of novels that break rules in the name of style. Cormac McCarthy is one author I admire who flouts convention, mixing direct and reported speech, eschewing punctuation around dialogue.

If you want to break the rules then you must be sure-footed and consistent. Readers, publishers and agents might then accept it as style, or not. To begin it's best to play safe.

The rules of writing are about what not to do: don't over-write, don't tell when you can show, don't use clichés, I could go on. There is an excellent book called *How NOT to Write a Novel: 200 Mistakes to avoid at All Costs if You Ever Want to Get Published* by Mittelmark and Newman. I can highly recommend it for an entertaining take on the most common new author writing mistakes as observed by literary agents and publishers. Mittelmark and Newman's listed pitfalls are something you have to learn through writing. They're part of the heavy pack that you must carry up Kilimanjaro.

Here follows my take on the rules, a lighter set of guidelines, survival rations for the trek. They're not exhaustive and quite subjective, based on my views as an author, reviewer and reader.

Plot and premise

This is the cornerstone upon which you build your novel. A foundation must be sure and true because everything stands upon it. The plot also pretty much defines the genre and gives you your novel tagline:

- man saves unknown woman from becoming a murder victim – crime fiction;

- leper falls unconscious and wakes in a strange land to find he has special powers – fantasy;

- last outpost of the human race comes under threat of annihilation by aliens – science fiction;

- young boy reaches high school age and finds out he's a wizard – YA fantasy;

and so on.

The premise can be fantastic but it must be believable. Your job is to suspend disbelief.

Stephen King, in his *On Writing*, calls plot *the good writer's last resort and the dullard's first choice. The story which results from it is apt to feel artificial and labored.* He only goes as far as to place one or more characters in a predicament and watch them try to work themselves free. King takes an intuitive approach and merely observes what happens, writing it down. That approach has obviously been successful for his type of writing.

I'm not going to give you a definitive guide to the seven basic plots or variant thereupon, although there are books that do that (see Recommended Reading). If you can describe in one sentence (your *Elevator Pitch*) what your story is, then you have your plot cornerstone. Where you go from there depends upon your approach to planning.

Planning and structure

You have your plot premise. Now what are you going to do with it?

Here are some characteristic planning approaches as food for thought.

The General plans a novel with military precision. The protagonist has landed in a predicament and must make choices. Those choices have consequences beyond the actions themselves. Circumstances and an antagonist conspire to frustrate the main character's plan and the story races towards success or failure of the mission. A chart stretches around all the walls of your study and maps out each chapter, layering tension upon tension until the eventual climax. If you have your complete plot in your head and the only hindrance is getting it down on paper, then this is for you.

The Puzzler articulates a premise and then writes the final chapter, or even the final line. The rest is a journey through the maze, urging the main character to survive a catalogue of trials and tribulations in pursuit of the intended outcome. A lyric by Talking Heads springs to mind: *We know where we're going, but we don't know where we've been.* This approach relies upon the author's trust in their self, that they can bring their main character through the rain to safe haven.

The Allotment Grower considers the premise as more of a seed than a cornerstone and lets the thing grow organically, making occasional sanity checks along the way. There is no preconceived ending. The author is as surprised as the reader with the denouement. This approach is a dare to dream, translating subconscious intuition into ninety thousand words. The risk here is that things will go awry and the first draft will require substantial analysis and rewrite. I am that soldier.

Do you recognise your preferred approach to planning in any of the above? If your novel is going to be character driven, rather than plot driven, then the emphasis is going to be on your literary writing skills. If you're ready for that, then great. If not, then have a plot, use your personal approach to planning and on with the novel, for life is short.

Characters

The story is taking shape so let's meet your characters. Every novel has characters. Like a film, there are leading roles, supporting cast and extras. Your job is to engage the reader in the experiences and emotions of the leading roles.

Those that have the story told from their perspective (see Narrative Voice below) tend to be the main characters. The good guy is the protagonist, the bad guy the antagonist. Of course, things aren't always black and white. Your main character may be an anti-hero or an underdog. You might even take the bad lad as your main character.

New authors often make mistakes with characterisation, such as:

Pop-up characters - the main characters are described in adequate detail, ideally through their actions and words, but other characters are cardboard cut-outs that stand by the wayside as the plot trundles past. This is what reviewers mean when they say your characters are two-dimensional. Think of the pop-up figures that feature in those shooting ranges where the gun wielding trainee has to decide which are the bad guys that need shooting and the good guys that need saving.

He took a long and loving look at his reflection - characters are introduced with a snapshot description, like a pin-on set of doll clothes. A device is often used such as they catch their reflection in a shop window or a mirror, else another character describes them as they appear. I recently read a novel where every character was introduced in this way, like a Penney's radio advertisement for clothes. Unless you're a fashionista this can be a real drag. It presses the pause button while the complete ensemble is described. The character is now three-dimensional but hollow, a mannequin.

Angels and demons - the protagonist is improbably virtuous, an angel thinking only pure thoughts and behaving impeccably. The antagonist is Dr Evil, their twisted deeds driven by inhuman motivation. Side characters talk and behave in ways convenient for the plot. In reality, nobody's behaviour is black or white. All real people are a shade of grey, they aren't caricatures. Even serial killers are somebody's son, or daughter.

Clone wars - there is no discernable difference in the language that the characters use when they speak, the way they think and move, the way they react to the plot as it unfurls. The reader starts to become confused about who is who. In extreme cases the characters even have names that are too similar – Dr Liffey, Mike Caffey, John McCaffrey, Laura Casey. In real life people are diverse and instantly recognisable by their voices, the way they walk, habits of speech and behaviour, and so on.

I find that once I'm laughing, crying, despairing, feeling pain and celebrating with my characters they have come to life. A tutor of mine says authors should have conversations out loud with their characters. (If you decide to try this method then I suggest not to do it in a public place, especially on a train!) Write out one page of who the character is, how they look (including clothes), what they've done and plan to do, their characteristics of speech and their typical behaviour. This confirms that the character is a real person and allows you to articulate the mechanical details without listing them in your novel. Drop incidental details in as part of narrative or dialogue. *He hitched up his jeans by the belt loop. It was the third time she'd seen him do it that evening.*

Narrative voice

Who is telling this story? Well, I know you, the author, are writing the story but whose voice are we hearing in our heads when we read?

All-knowing – the omniscient narrator is a supreme being who knows what everyone is thinking and doing all the time. This is the ultimate fly-on-the-wall and permits the story to head hop at will. The danger is, in the wrong hands, omniscient is obsessed with detail, leaves no mystery and doesn't let the reader identify strongly with key characters.

He, she, they – third person is a limited form of omniscient where the author is detached from the characters and doesn't know what everyone is thinking, doing or has done. This can lead to a high degree of detachment from the story and characters as it's purely observational. What is more normal is to have a limited third person viewpoint where the story is told in a he / she / they fashion, giving the narrator all the knowledge, emotions and experiences of the viewpoint character. The author might also, from time to time, change the character whose viewpoint is taken (this usually involves a new chapter).

I, me, follow me – first person narrator makes the story teller the main character, usually the protagonist. Everything is told from the knowledge, emotions and ongoing experiences of that person. This approach puts the reader right inside the head of that viewpoint character. That's a good thing as long as it's a bearable place to be. First person is asking the reader to empathise to some extent with the character, running the risk that not all readers will be comfortable with that. It's also possible to change the character whose viewpoint is taken but, with first person, each character must have a distinct and unique voice. First person runs the risk of monologue with a leading 'I' (I did this, I saw that, I had a cup of tea), so a very healthy smattering of dialogue is advised to avoid that pitfall. Also watch out for the tendency of first person narrator to produce a linear story.

You, yes you, pay attention – second person narrator is rare. The narrative voice is the main character / observer addressing either the reader or some fictitious person as though they were speaking or writing directly to them. For example, Aravind Adiga's *White Tiger* uses second person by addressing a visiting dignitary in a series of letters. Practically, second person can't be maintained otherwise it's like someone reading a statement of events to you. The narrative usually slips into the first person.

The dodgy geezer, or unreliable narrator, is worth a mention. First and second person narrators provide the individual viewpoints, perceptions and opinions of the characters. Unlike omniscient (assuming we trust the omnipotent) and third person (again assumption of objective honesty), the first or second person may have reason to be economical with the truth or even has a different lens on reality compared with the rest of humanity. This can give us an unreliable narrator and that unreliability is usually then a key aspect of the premise and plot.

Tense

Premise, plot and characters are decided. You've chosen the voice(s) to tell the story. So, when did this all happen? Or is it happening now? A key decision is whether to report the main action of your story in past or present tense.

Once upon a time, in a Galaxy far, far away. Past tense is the most common. It has a relaxed, reported feel to it, a tale being retold by the narrator. It's a natural way of telling a story and almost all of the verbs are conjugated with 'ed', so easy writing.

I can feel his hot breath on my neck. Present tense plunges the reader into the timeline. This can be very useful for novels that are full of tension. The reader is in the room where the action is happening, either watching the characters or actually doing whatever the narrative character is doing. One of the pitfalls of present tense is that the author may be tempted to describe every single action and this can lead to the mundane occupying too much space on the page. I recently read a novel where the...no, I can't tell you. Sufficient to say, it was a toilet scene. Present is also the tense most readers find tiresome over the length of a novel.

Mix and match. Present and past tense can be mixed. For example, the contemporary narrative may be present tense and flashbacks given in past tense. It's also possible to give flashbacks in present tense: *Last week I'm queuing at the supermarket checkout and some bloke stands so close behind me I can feel his hot breath on my neck*. This kind of mix and match is okay as long as the reader doesn't become confused as to the timeline.

Narrative voice + tense combo

The combined choice of who is telling the story and when it is happening will have a major impact upon the reading experience. First person present tense is perhaps the most challenging but it places the reader behind the eyes of the main character as events occur. Third person past tense is the default mode, a safer option for holding the reader's attention.

Settings – the six senses

Okay, so you have your premise, some idea of how the plot will develop, who the key players are and how the story is going to be told. Now, to make this fictional world come alive, the settings must be made real. You need to switch on your senses and see, hear, touch, taste and smell the location, but without overt description if possible. Your sixth sense is often the best way to describe the setting – how does it feel? (But note that use of *it feels like* is not the way to do it either. The reader has to sense without being told.)

A typical beginner's mistake is to introduce the setting by looking through the character's eyes and simply repeating what they see e.g.

a thirty foot hallway, dirty beige carpet and a window at the far end approximately two feet off the ground, one foot wide and three feet in height, peeling paint and dirty glass. The house looks uncared for.

It's better to let the character's actions, thoughts and words give the setting detail indirectly e.g.

He didn't worry about the mess his boots made on the carpet. It was difficult to tell where the pattern finished and the stains started.

Pace & structure

There are novels you want to read in a day, consuming page after page at great pace, driven by the desire to find out what happens. There are novels which can be picked up and put down, chapters standing alone as short stories or episodes in themselves. And of course there are shades in between. Either way, the reader interest is maintained and the author brings them along on the journey at a deliberate pace.

Your novel can have a linear structure but, unless you deliver it skilfully, many readers will find boring a chronological storyline that accompanies the protagonist through their trials and tribulations. More often than not the story needs to move through different times and places, providing back-story where appropriate so the reader understands why people are behaving the way they do and what has transpired to produce certain events. You might also have parallel threads running in the story which should hopefully converge at some point.

Chapter breaks are often difficult to call. I'm a writer of relatively short chapters but each one has a start initiated by some change in the story such as time, setting and / or narrator. I also like to give a hook at the end of each chapter to pull the reader on towards the next. As I write in first person, usually with an unreliable narrator, the style can be staccato. One online critic advised me to go read some books on structure, yet the same novel opening went on to be a prize winner without any structural changes. That's the risk with style; it won't be to everybody's taste.

If you want to be 'normal' then a chapter of around three thousand words would be my suggestion.

Dialogue – people will talk

It isn't easy to write good dialogue. That's one reason many authors try to avoid it. The result of too little dialogue is a long narrative that can end up more like a monologue than a novel.

When people speak in real life they rarely talk in a grammatically correct fashion. A lot of words are abbreviated and sentences left unfinished. Speech mannerisms are widespread, such as the interrogative tone, right? And people often start verbal sentences with *and*, and ending with *like*, like. These last two sentences look strange in narrative but would be perfectly acceptable in dialogue, where grammar rules are put on pause.

Dialogue should be written so it sounds natural.

'*Do not tell me that is the wrong way. You are not helping.*' This sounds over-articulated and stilted. Some people do speak like that but they're mostly members of the British Royal Family.

'*Don't tell me that's the wrong way. You're not helping.*' This is more typical of normal speech.

Try reading your dialogue out loud or listen to it with a text-to-speech programme. Any unrealistic dialogue will be immediately apparent.

However, there are a few limitations that should be placed on natural dialogue.

The stumbling mumbler. Er, um, ah and also...overuse of...ellipses. Natural speech contains a lot of pauses and incoherent conjunctions. Dialogue in a novel should contain few, if any, of these. This is a case where what goes unremarked in actual speech is awkward when read.

The st-st-st-stuttering listhp. Speech impediments can affect almost anyone, especially when under pressure. We're all instantly recognised by our voices and it's a great talent to be able to mimic voices accurately, but don't try and do it in your novel's dialogue. Slang, turns of phrase, abbreviations are all good, but trying to constantly imitate a stutter or a lisp will soon annoy readers.

'Awrigh geeza, wotcha gunna gis fur dinna?' Mimicking accents with phonetics is another danger zone. If a character speaks in a broad Cockney or Glaswegian accent then their dialogue in real life would be incomprehensible to most people, so there's no point trying to reproduce it. I recently reviewed a novel that had a main character speak in a Southern US drawl (which is fine, I like the accent too) but everything was spelt phonetically. After soldiering through fifty pages I had to give up.

What can work, in both of the above cases, is if a character has a very small share of the dialogue, and their accent or impediment is key to the story. Otherwise it's best left alone.

'You're a left-handed architect,' Holmes extrapolated. Speech tags are tempting. They let the author tell the reader so much more, right? Wrong. They tend to over-explain the intended mood and tone of the dialogue. *Said* is usually a perfectly adequate speech tag and it should come after the speaker's name. Put it before and the result is a bit self-conscious, as in children's books. Occasionally it may be a good idea to use a tag that describes the manner of the speech, if it's not obvious e.g. *whispered*.

If the dialogue voices of the characters are sufficiently distinctive, and there are just one or two people speaking, you might dispense with tags altogether. Shouted dialogue usually carries an exclamation mark and rarely needs a tag.

'Do you mean to say that we have been friends since childhood?' There is often a temptation to use dialogue as a vehicle to impart further information to the reader, information that the speakers of that dialogue already know and would never actually say to each other. Watch out for this. Even if the wording of the dialogue is perfect, the explanatory nature of its content will make it ridiculous and throw the reader out of the groove.

There are a few key new author dialogue punctuation mistakes that are worth a mention and tend to be systemically right or wrong in an individual's work.

'Hand me that bill. I mean hand me that, Bill.' If the speaker uses the name of the person they're speaking to then a comma is needed before the name (to avoid confusion).

'He's your dad, Dad.' When a word is used as a proper noun (Dad) then a capital is required. When used as a noun (someone's dad) then no capital.

'You need to close with a comma.' He said something else... If dialogue is given a speech tag then the dialogue should close with a comma. If there isn't a tag but a statement e.g. *He stood up* then the dialogue should close with a full stop.

Theme - metaphor

If you intend for your novel to make a statement about fate, the human condition or some other philosophical aspect, then that's admirable. If you don't set out with that intention then don't be too concerned. The components mentioned above will give you the content that you need. Many times I've heard or read interviews of famous authors during which an ardent fan will ask how the author chose their apparent theme and had the fan correctly understood what they were trying to say between the lines. In more cases than not the author laughs with slight embarrassment and says that they're very flattered by the fan's interpretation, but they weren't trying to send a message to the world. They just wrote the novel that was in their head.

When the reviews started to come in for my first novel I began to realise that there were themes in my story. The reviews helped me understand the appeal of the book and what readers took from it. I knew these things intuitively but hadn't articulated them. It's been a learning curve for me, as an author, to be helped by readers in better understanding what I've written. I'm just not that clever.

Your theme is implicit in your premise and plot. If you explicitly articulate that theme then be careful not to overcook it because if you do then, like roast turkey, it may become very dry.

Language and grammar

Dot your eyes and cross your tees. If you pick up *The Mayor of Casterbridge* by Thomas Hardy, *Catcher in the Rye* by J.D. Salinger and *Trainspotting* by Irvine Welsh, they all have something in common. All the words therein are spelt correctly and consistently. There are sentences with beginnings and ends. Capital letters and punctuation are consistent and correct. You'll also notice slight variations in the interpretation of what is correct grammar and punctuation, because these things can flex according to author style and the period of writing.

An author can pretty much get away with almost anything in the name of style as long as they remain consistent but, as a new author, it's safer to stick to the basic rules.

Would you please pass me a rubber? I need to erase something. You may have noticed spelling mistakes in what you've read so far. If that's the case then you are probably a user of American English. As a Brit living in Ireland I use UK English and the obvious impact of that is to include the letter 'u' in some words and use 's' instead of 'z' in others. But there's much more to it than that. Objects have different names in different countries. Excuse me while I get the maiden out of the airing cupboard. Even that sentence changes completely between Northern England and Ireland. Scissors is plural in England and singular in Ireland. Then there are idioms, turns of phrase and slang that are particular to countries, regions or even cities. We are all separated by a common language.

So, what to do? Remember *A Clockwork Orange* by Anthony Burgess. The language used is a future-speak that is unique to the dystopian time and place of the story. That's the key. Your language should be appropriate to the narrative voice, the characters and the setting of your novel.

Comma coma. There are rules for commas. Some folks follow those rules exactly, their only variance being whether or not they invoke the Oxford comma. *Eats, Shoots and Leaves* by Lynne Truss is a very good guide to proper use. Classical literature includes a comma with every hesitation, each pause for breath, and any discontinuity in the sentence clause. I used to write like that and found that, when submitting work to creative writing classes, my pieces were awash with commas. I began to doubt my hard learned comma capabilities and felt like a dinosaur falling into an Ice Age coma. So I turned to a more intuitive approach.

The intuitive rule I adopted is what I call the kids' reading rule. If my seven year-old son reads the words I have written with the cadence that I intended, pausing slightly at each comma, then it's right. Using a text-to-speech facility is an easier way than getting a child to read a full adult novel. It's a very useful trick for final edits.

Cliché corner. It's time to *wipe the slate clean, turn over a new leaf* and *just do it. Yes, we can.* It's tempting, comfortable and familiar to speak in well-used parlance. TV shows and advertising rely upon the appeal of tag lines. However, the overuse of phrases eventually wears their originality away like the gold plate on a cheap watch.

This became clear to me when, after seven years abroad, I returned to the UK and walked into my own wedding party full of people who were talking in a language that meant nothing to me. I could hear the words strung together, everybody speaking from the same stock phrases that soon lost meaning after the first time heard. There had been a run of successful TV comedy shows and the conversation mostly consisted of catchphrase regurgitation.

The great radio shows of yesteryear were the origin of many of our more obscure turns of phrase. Catchphrases, jargon and rhetoric share a common attribute. They have all become clichéd and lost their original power of meaning through overuse.

Clichés abound in some styles of novel – romance and YA tend to favour them – but are otherwise best avoided. If you find yourself writing a cliché then stop, consider what you want to convey and then try and write it in a more original way that suits the narrative voice. There are some circumstances where clichés do fit. In dialogue people should speak naturally and that will inevitably involve an amount of overused phrases. Another case is first person narrator, if the voice is one that tends to use clichés.

Adverb adversity. The contemporary wisdom is that adverbs show a weakness in the writing. The manner in which an action is carried out or the way something is spoken should be obvious from the author's word-craft. That said, children's fiction is happily awash with adverbs, and classics are colourfully painted with them.

Less is more (isn't that a cliché?) Yes, it is. In fact, most advice runs the risk of cliché, but this is a good piece of advice. I know writers that can write a sparkling, succinct and original sentence. Breathtaking. Then, either from lack of confidence that the message has been got over or to add emphasis, they layer another gold star sentence on top. Why not then add a third, and more follow. The result is that the sum of the parts is less than one piece of the whole (I think that counts as a butchered cliché).

An author's over-writing problem often comes to the fore when emotion is described in increasing layers of intensity. It can form a vortex that sucks the narrative off course e.g. from romance to horror. She was hurt. Hurt so bad. It felt like her self-esteem had fallen through a trap-door. Tumbling deep into an abyss of self-doubt, beyond the reach of even the strongest light. To the depths of despair's ocean where translucent night-dwellers feasted upon the lost souls of despair. Hopelessness and howling her only companions. Then a darkness descended, the world was black, an emotional apocalypse etc. Or maybe you actually like that? If so, fair enough.

Show not tell (isn't that another cliché?) Yes, it is, and ditto the above. As soon as the author tells the reader how a character is feeling, what they are doing, what the setting looks like, then the author is being too obvious, too explicit. They don't trust the reader to get it and begin to patronise. The effect is to detach a reader, to move them into observation of the story rather than have them live it. The difference can be small. *She was sad* versus *a tear rolled down her cheek*. From the tear rolling a reader can divine that the character is sad (depending upon the chopped onions situation).

Back-up – frequently

I've included this in The Rules because, although it's not a creative writing rule, it has to be in your mind at all times. There will be grinding of teeth and tearing of hair in the households of authors that don't keep back-ups of everything. This applies to more than just your treasured manuscript. These days everything is embedded in technology. Laptops, netbooks and tablets. Websites, blogs and web-based email. All of these things end up containing hundreds of thousands of words that have come, through your keyboard, via your fingers, originating in your mind. Expect this technology to fail, because it will. Anticipate obsolescence, because it's going to happen. In order to avoid tears you must back-up your written words and images and all moments of brilliance. Version control is also paramount. More about this later.

Title

If you achieve a mainstream publishing deal then there's a strong likelihood that a title will be chosen for you and the name in which you had poured out your soul is relegated to 'working title'. As an independent author you get to choose the title under which your novel will be published. Wield this privilege with care.

I had a 'great' title for my first novel. The Rise and Fall of Ger Mayes. It was a play upon the title of a slightly alternative BBC TV comedy programme that was popular in Britain about thirty years ago. The main character was always late for work, blaming improbable excuses such as a rampaging herd of wildebeest. He frequently imagined his mother-in-law as a hippopotamus wallowing in mud. Hilarious, so I thought. I did so chuckle at my own cleverness, reminding people that my dark humour was of a similar standard to an obscure British TV comedy. Unfortunately I was alone in my mirth and it took some very good friends to tell me that the title was a turkey. *Not the snappiest of titles* was how one renowned journalist and crime author described it. The novel has done much better under the new title *Peril* and it sums up the premise of the novel – a man who places himself, friends and family in peril through a catalogue of bad decisions.

Getting done – good enough

The curse of the unfinished symphony. I've never had a problem in producing volumes of words, verbally or on the page. Well, until I discovered social media but that story comes later. Once I put my mind to it, things get done. There's a fairly uninterrupted connection between my thoughts and fingertips and I'm lucky in that way. Not everyone is the same.

People take different paths to find their way towards writing a novel. Flash fiction, blog posts, articles, short stories, novellas or straight into the full-length book. It's all good and there will be times when one or another form best suits how you're thinking and what is going on in your life. A spontaneous blog post that takes half an hour. A literary novel that takes eight years. The most important thing, in all cases, is to get done. Complete, finish, and produce a result.

I've met people in writing groups who have started tens of short stories and finished none. If getting finished is a problem you suffer from then peer group support is crucial for you.

Editing

Completion of a novel is a great satisfaction in itself. Celebrate that achievement and then put the book aside for a period of time, from a couple of weeks to a couple of months if you can stand it. Start another project, keep writing, but let your completed manuscript be for a while. When you come back to it, you do so as a reader instead of author and you'll have a much more objective take on what works and what doesn't.

So, putting on your editor's hat, what should you be looking for? *Self-Editing for Fiction Writers* by Renni Browne and Dave King is a very useful book that contains detailed guidance including checklists, exercises and techniques for editing your novel into shape. The chapter headings of the book (e.g. Show and Tell, Characterization and Exposition, Point of View) reveal editing for what it really is. Editing is the process of realigning your novel with best practice. You read your work through, compare it with The Rules and then adjust as best you can.

How you accomplish this task depends upon what works for you. Here are some characteristic approaches.

The Reiterator likes to edit on the hoof whilst writing the manuscript. S/he writes a paragraph, reads back the paragraph, adjusts, rereads, tweaks. Once the manuscript first draft is finished, *The Reiterator* may feel that the job is complete. Nevertheless, a holistic view is needed in editing that first draft to ensure that the perfect pieces of the jigsaw meld well together. A disadvantage of *The Reiterator* is completion of the first draft can take a very, very long time compared to other approaches which are more tolerant of imperfection.

The Salami Slicer takes a knife to the manuscript and severs slices of less than perfect writing according to each of *The Rules*. *The Salami Slicer* places the narrative voice hat upon their head and reads the manuscript through for consistent and appropriate narrative point of view, adjusting as necessary. Then the dialogue hat is donned, the show-not-tell hat and so on. This approach means a new read through for every rule but is very thorough. One pitfall is *The Salami Slicer* can become fixated on a particular aspect of *The Rules* and overdo the editing. For example, the word *that* is often overused by new authors and can be eliminated unless essential for the meaning of a sentence, but such a narrow focus can lead to a mechanical approach and leave readers tripping over sentences where *that* is actually needed but has been cut.

The Jack of All Trades applies all the rules at once as s/he reads through the manuscript, spotting discontinuities, point of view slips, structural and grammatical problems etc. as they arise. This is the fastest and most holistic way to edit but requires a high degree of alertness and flexibility.

The Listener prefers to hear the manuscript read aloud. A traditional *Listener* will lock themselves away and read the book out loud to themselves, but the 21st century *Listener* uses a text-to-speech facility on their e-reading device or laptop. There are numerous text-to-speech voices and accents available free on the web, but even the robotic default MS voices do a good job of exposing missing commas, word echo, unintentional alliteration and stilted or unnatural dialogue. A good *Listener* can sense, from the cadence of spoken word, the mood and emotions of the piece. That's if they can concentrate and stay awake for the duration of the reading.

The Outsourcer wants to be done with the manuscript once the first draft is completed and have a third party (sometimes more than one) take care of slapping the novel into shape. Depending upon the level of financial investment you are willing to make, this may be an option. Some novel writing books advocate passing your manuscript through the hands of different types of editor e.g. developmental, copy, proofreading. The advantage of this is you can whisk your manuscript off to the third party as soon as it's finished, no time wasted. The disadvantage is the author doesn't gain the learning themselves from having self-edited. In addition, editors can't make a silk purse out of a sow's ear. If, as an independent author, you do want to outsource your editing then you need an element of confidence that your writing has reached a level that makes paid-for editing worthwhile.

Self-editing is a learning experience. Being able to spot what works and what doesn't, and learning how to fix the deficiencies, eventually leads to an increased sophistication in the author's writing. These skills can be further developed by participating in writing groups where you will also have the opportunity to edit the work of others.

Writing peer groups

Being an author is a fundamentally solitary occupation. Like all hermits, we can get a little crazy now and then. This might manifest itself in our writing.

If you want to write a good novel as a new author then, in almost all cases, you need to build your experience of writing. Reading books on writing is one good step in the right direction. There will come a time when you might consider working with other people – a tutor, or mentor, and other writers.

Creative writing courses are run in most cities and many large towns. Some colleges also run online courses. It's a good idea to acquire a sound knowledge of the fundamentals of creative writing and such a course should provide you with that, as well as an interactive peer group and hopefully a supportive and nurturing tutor. If a writing course does appeal to you then make sure to study the curriculum carefully and try to speak with previous students so you can gauge whether the course deliverables, style of teaching and workload are a good match for your expectations.

The ultimate objective of every writer is to find their writing voice, to effortlessly express their stories in an individual style that delights readers. Reaching that objective can be a rollercoaster ride of discovery and doubt, growing confidence and setbacks, obscurity and recognition. A good course tutor will lead pupils from their initial condition of unconscious incompetence towards the goal of conscious competence. The course attendees will develop strong, dependent team relationships through group work and critique of each other's writing. It's not uncommon for the nucleus of the group to continue after the course is ended, meeting periodically and maintaining the momentum that was established when learning together.

Writing groups are a good source of peer group interaction. Typical activities might include regular submissions for group critique, discussion of writing challenges the individuals are facing, upcoming competitions, sharing of new writing resources that members have discovered etc. The submission and critique aspect of a writing group is highly valuable and, over time, the bulk of a novel might be dealt with. However, care has to be taken that mutual trust and respect exists and is maintained within the group, that all criticism remains objective and constructive, and that the principles underlying the critique rationale are sound.

Online writing groups are an alternative approach with some advantages and disadvantages over a physical writing group.

On the plus side:

- you don't have to physically be there, so it's well-suited to people who live in a geographically remote location and all you need is an internet connection;

- there's no cost involved;

- you set the pace of review of your work;

- you will build a network of online author friends and can pick up lots of useful information regarding online resources, social networking and publishing;

- there is a possibility (whatever the odds) that an agent or publisher will spot your work;

- you can review a lot of different styles and genres and you will learn a lot from the large volume of critiques that you will write.

On the minus side:

- it can be addictive – okay, not clinically addictive but it can and usually does lead to a degree of compulsive behaviour;

- if your internet connection is unreliable or goes down then you will be climbing the walls with frustration;

- members that review your work are not necessarily trained in creative writing, so their judgement and advice is sometimes misguided;

- it can be difficult to take criticism constructively as a written critique is lacking

- in the interactive content of a face-to-face writers' group;

- if you dabble in the chat forums there are a host of other dangers – bullying, trolls, flame wars – a lot of self-control is needed not to get caught up in the microcosm of a virtual community;

- not everyone has the confidence, self-discipline, diplomacy or thick skin required for online peer review groups.

There will come a time when you, as an author, find your writing voice. Everything you produce hits a sweet spot and the writing group becomes a mutual appreciation society. At that point, or thereabouts, it might be appropriate to leave behind the world of writing groups or at least withdraw from peer group critique.

Beta readers

Your manuscript is complete. It's been critiqued, partially or totally, by your writing group and put through the editing process of your choice. You're twitching to unleash this novel upon the world but, apart from you and maybe an editor, no one has actually read the thing as it was intended, as a continuous work. You don't have a literary agent and publishing house reassuring you that the novel is ready to market because you've bravely chosen the ebook revolution route of independent publishing. The first reactions to your novel are going to be from those initial purchasers who feel strongly enough to write a review online. Will they love it, or will they hate it? There is a way to test the water; beta readers. A beta reader is someone who reads a book prior to its release to the general public.

The second part of this book will help you develop a broad writer's network through social media. You will be able to find beta readers from within this network and also possibly from your writers group. There may be a friend or colleague from your non-author circles that you want to invite as a beta reader. If you do then make sure you choose someone who is a regular reader, ideally in the genre that you're aiming for. This sounds like a no-brainer but it's surprising how many people foist their first novels upon unwilling and embarrassed family or friends who might not even be part of their target demographic. There's a risk of being damned by faint praise (a cliché that fits well here) when the reader feels obligated to be nice.

With your beta reader(s) selected, ask them to read your novel as they would any other. Ideally give them the novel as a Word doc or printed copy so they have the option to type or write their thoughts straight into the story as they go through it. If you have nagging doubts about some aspects of your novel (e.g. authenticity of settings, believability of plot, reader sympathy for the protagonist) then pose those questions after the reading. Thank the beta reader for their feedback and carefully consider if you want to make any changes based upon their input.

You're novel has now been read as intended and, if they've enjoyed it and are comfortable with sharing their opinions on the internet, your beta readers may be the source of your first book reviews.

Reading will never be the same again

I've made the assumption that, as an aspiring author, you are also a prolific reader. If you're not then you should become one. Use any spare leisure time you have to pick up and read novels in print or ebook format. During breakfast, on the bus, tea-break, wherever you can, whenever you're not writing creatively. Now that you are aware of the components of fiction writing, it will become more apparent to you why some novels work for you as a reader and why some don't. It's as if you have acquired a minor superpower but the bad news is you can't turn it off at will. You will read novels with a critical eye forevermore. If you find yourself at the end of a novel without being critical of the writing then that is your ideal novel.

Using this new special power, select your reading a little more carefully and explore genres, read and study bestsellers, seek out examples of different narrative voice and maybe try some stylised rule-breaking reading while you're at it. There are some great reader websites (see the Goodreads and LibraryThing sections in Part 2 of this book) where you can discuss with other readers and authors about books within genres. This activity can also be crafted into your social networking platform where you will present yourself both as an author and a reader.

We'll close this section with a vignette (quaint word) about the perils of online writing groups and peer review.

~~~

Vignette 1 - Peer review; the blind leading the blind?

Originally written as a guest post for multi-story.co.uk, the chosen guest subject was one close to my heart - the trials and tribulations of writers that cut their teeth in the ether of peer review writing websites. I was that soldier. Delighted to say that one elephant joke was allowed. Here's the article...

Except for the lucky few, we've all been there: typed the closing lines of our first completed work of fiction; sighed with contentment; packaged the manuscript in a glossy folder depicting dolphins or kittens; anointed the query letter with a dab of perfume and presented Mrs Murphy at the Post Office with half a dozen packets of literary heaven.

'Yes, Mrs Murphy, all this time, living in your midst, like a normal person. I am a writer!' (Adopts mincing stride and a flourish of the hand).

Next day's walk to work is on air, knowing that there won't be many more such mundane days because the agent, publisher and film producer will be in a bare-knuckle fight over who will make the most money from your blockbusting masterpiece now winging its way to the literary world.

A few celebratory bottles of wine and several days later the self-satisfaction of the perfectly packaged bundles is wearing off. A couple of weeks and you decide to redecorate walls of your study with all the rejection slips that begin to flood through the letterbox like Hogwarts invitations arriving at the Dursleys'. Clearly the agents and publishers you selected weren't selected carefully enough. Might the action adventure of a philandering power generation engineer's international swashbuckling be a little out of their genre? Writers and Artists Year Book in hand, you print another batch of submissions, make a mad dash to the stationers and endure sweaty tussles with other anguished authors over the last remaining large Jiffy bag. Another few weeks and a second wall of the study gets papered with the next wave of responses.

The logical next step presents itself. Consult an expert. Hand over a tidy sum of money to a professional third party in return for a critique of the manuscript, to try and understand why the rejections keep coming. A nice little man, with a peculiar talent for acidity, points out that characters, plot, pace & structure, use of language, narrative voice (what's that?), dialogue, settings and theme are all awry. But the query letter is nicely fragrant. A discussion of these results with family and friends reveals that any number of them would have happily given you a similar kick in the privates for much less money than you paid to a stranger.

So, now you've been battered about the head with what is wrong with the masterwork, how do you put it right? A formal creative writing course is out of the question because you're broke / agoraphobic / living in the middle of nowhere / in a foreign country / in custody. A bit of internet research reveals that you are not alone. There are global communities of aspiring writers posting their work online, critiquing each other's efforts and striving to rise above the hoi polloi. Free-to-join websites run by reputable folk. Prizes of professional critique by editors from the big publishing houses. Success stories of authors that have been discovered and offered seven figure publishing contracts. You sign up, format your manuscript for online consumption and prepare for greatness. You are officially in a writers' group. Happy days.

What happens next depends upon the architecture of the peer review website. In any case, a burst of compulsive activity is likely. You are a newbie and, unless you are somehow familiar with online communities and forums, all those beginners' mistakes await you. Strangers will offer friendship. Strangers will crawl all over your literary masterpiece and tear the flesh from its bones. Internet trolls await, running out to engage you in flame wars of words if you should clop too loudly across their bridge.

You begin to gather feedback on the pages that you posted for virtual consumption. This involves a reciprocal arrangement with other writers, either in a structured one-for-one review system or through social networking. All of a sudden you're not just a writer; you're also a reader, a reviewer, a critic. Folk expect you to be able to constructively critique their work. You make mistakes, go with trends like less is more, show not tell, and where to stick your Oxford commas. You exchange writer jokes on message boards e.g. Marriage isn't a word, it's a sentence. LOL. Other acronyms such as POV and IMHO start to become part of your parlance. It's likely that you will regurgitate criticism, either acknowledging learning from the reviews that you've received or biting back at viewpoints and opinions that seem uninformed or spiteful.

Month three of online peer review and there aren't enough hours in the day, enough days in the week, to do enough reviews, to earn enough credits for reviews of your own work, to network friends, to climb the mountain of the charts and attain that Holy Grail of a pro-crit. Waves of self-doubt wash across your frontal lobe as your chart ranking fluctuates. Newbie reviewers play havoc with your scores as they deliver novice critique of your work. You start to frequent the discussion forum and find solace in the company of other authors, your seniority growing. Is first person, post-modernist narrative voice passé? Should you rewrite in a less florid or less minimalist style to elicit more favourable reviews from the peer group? There seems to be a hard-core clique that knows the secrets to all this, the mechanism of the charts and how to spam to the top without being seen to spam. It's a tough time, you're not getting anything written except reviews of other people's work and you're neglecting the ironing.

Month six and you've become a firm member of the old guard. Respected by veterans, dissed by paranoid newbies, considered a part of that alleged clique. Your revised work is doing well and it's on final ascent to the summit of the charts. Your extended social network is brought into play, posting support requests on facebook, twitter and every form of social media known to authors and readers. The last day of the month approaches, there's a photo finish, a Steward's appeal and yes, you're a winner! High fives all round, virtual back-slapping and emoticons [sic] aplenty on the forum.

The long wait begins. Will the professional critique confirm your writing skill, honed by crash-course experience in the intense editing and critiquing world of online peers? In the interim, you arse about on the forum, see off a few trolls and grace a few newbies with gratis reviews and critiques. Just for fun you designate a particular aspect of creative writing as your special focus area for the day, using Mittelmark & Newman's *How Not to Write a Novel* as your bible.

On Mondays you severely and mercilessly critique a piece, soundly and resolutely thrashing it for excessive use of adverbs.

Tuesdays are an attack on two-dimensional characters, asking that they be fleshed out so that they leap from the page.

Wednesdays you add a little extra, advising the writer to titillate the senses by making sure that all settings are a tasteful olfactory, tactile, audiovisual experience.

Thursdays are the day to attack any speech tag other than 'said'.

Friday is for fish and you go angling for inadvertent red herrings that mislead the reader.

Saturday deals with the identity parade syndrome, taking down an author or two that uses a mirror or other blatant device to give a photo-fit description of characters with big dark eyes, silken hair, a matching twin-set in cornflower blue and average size breasts.

Sunday you weed out the clichés from a newbie's work and leave them with the bare bones of a plot that then magically takes on the tone of a Scandinavian detective drama.

You've discovered the power to weave straw into gold. Your username is by now widely known on the site and has a well-earned reputation for being firm but fair. Empowered by the journey, it's time to launch new forum discussion threads about the fine differences between similes and metaphors, the plausibility of hyperbole, and to draw attention to an outbreak of anthropomorphism in the newbie writings you have come across. Wikipedia serves you particularly well in the formulation of your position on these matters.

At last the professional critique of your novel opening chapters arrives online. Some jumped-up junior editor from a big publishing house has totally panned your labour of love. Two-dimensional characters. The plot premise is unbelievable. Stilted dialogue. Over-described, over-told, indefinite genre, unmarketable. It has to be a mistake. The reviewer must have read a different book to the one that tens, hundred of people have voted for with their virtual feet. You followed their suggestions to the letter, those experienced online authors with knowledge of narrative voice, point of view, story arcs, prologues, scene, sequels, antagonists, conflict, protagonist, sensory perception. The result was almost edible and some young know-nothing has regurgitated it in your face, in public, for thousands of peers to see. Well, she's obviously wrong. To hell with the dead-tree publishers. You go straight to Kindle Direct Publishing and begin to upload your novel as an independent e-book. That'll show them.

I'll finish with a parable. Six blind men were asked to describe an elephant by touching its body. One felt the tail and said that the elephant was like a hairy rope. Another grasped a leg and said that it resembled a tree. A third handled the ear and was sure that it was a great flying bat. The fourth was snuffled by the trunk and said that an elephant was a mighty snake, bigger than a python. The tusk was touched by another who claimed that it was surely a unicorn. The sixth found its huge eye and knew that it must be a giant squid. None of them could describe the hole. [sic]

~~~

RUBY BARNES

Part 2 - Promoting your brand by using social networks

Well, you have your novel in your hand and you're ready to go. Your social media networks are all up and running, right? No? In that case you're not ready to launch an ebook. So, to make sure you don't jump in at the deep end without the prerequisite aids, we have to thoroughly explore brand and product promotion using social networks.

I should mention not every successful ebook author uses social media networks. Some have such strong brands already that their name is enough to ensure ebook sales. But look into any independent ebook author on Amazon and you'll invariably find they have a solid social networking platform. In order to sell your book you need exposure and, as a new unknown author, this is the best foot forward.

Yes, I'm afraid the issue of marketing has to rear its Medusa head if you don't want your writing to languish in obscurity. And if it's ebooks you want to sell then your marketing efforts need to be internet based. The good news is almost anyone can build a marketing platform for ebooks just by following a few easy steps. It does take some time and there's a risk of compulsive behaviour.

Disclaimer! Technology is constantly evolving. This means that any assessment of social media is only a snapshot at the time of writing. So if I allude to the prevalence of facebook and twitter but both are dead and gone by the time you read this, then it's time for me to write a new edition.

What is a social media platform?

There are people who don't use the internet at all. You're not one of those but, for completeness, I'm going to assume (and yes, I know that to ASSUME makes an ASS out of U and ME) your knowledge of this stuff is as basic as mine was at the start.

Even if you only have an email address and a web browser (which you must have if you bought this book online) you are already engaging in social media networks. Any interaction with the web is like a stone thrown into a lake. For example, the simple fact of your buying an ebook on Amazon is fed into the network to inform features such as *customers who bought / viewed this item also bought*. If you write a review for the ebook then your username will be associated with that review, visible to other browsing customers and open to their comment. The author might link from twitter, facebook or their website to your review and it could even become part of a discussion on an Amazon chat forum in which you might be reviled or praised.

What I am going to explain is how to deliberately engage in selected social networks by building a platform of specific social networking tools. It's not difficult but first you need to stop and think.

Brand

The objective of marketing is to place your product with your target market, build your brand following, produce customer referrals and generate repeat sales for related products. The good news is marketing ebooks using social media can also be fun. As a starting point you need to decide upon your brand.

The best brand for an author is usually the name of that author. There are some exceptions, usually book series, where the brand strength lies in the titles (*Harry Potter* for example). Initially your readers will be buying your product title and not your author brand, but because you've written such an outstanding book, their loyalty will be to you, the author. Place the product successfully, establish the brand.

I'm emphasising this point right at the start because, as soon as you make the first step and register on a website for anything at all related to yourself as an author, the opportunity arises to do the right or the wrong thing with your brand. It's already happened. When you send me an email, what do I see in my inbox? You may have some kind of slightly preposterous handle to preserve your anonymity and amuse friends. My personal email is *turnip1962* but what you will see in your inbox is *Ruby Barnes*. That's an easy one to fix because the name that receivers of your mail see can be adjusted in your email settings. Other things are less easy to fix. Look at these examples from my disastrous first steps:

- first website *markturnerbooks.com* (I bought the URL, it can't be changed)

- first blog *markturnerbooks.blogspot.com* (registered, can't be changed)

- peer review website username *Turnip* (won two online prizes, can't be changed)

- facebook username *John Baptist* (one of my characters)

- Amazon Kindle Direct Publishing username *Ger Mayes* (can't be changed, name of one of my characters, this account has published my two ebooks).

This all happened because I knew nothing about building a social network platform and hadn't thought through my brand. Fortunately I bought and read a very useful book called *WANA* by Kristen Lamb and that helped me get back on track.

Nom de Plume?

As I state in my bio, Ruby Barnes was my Scottish grandfather's name. It might sound like a girl's name to you, but he looked like Popeye. I have my reasons for choosing to use a pen name, and I'm not suggesting that it's the right move for everyone, but the key point is that I was undecided about my brand. What I didn't internalise at the start was that every interaction I have with readers, writers and media as an author needs to consistently reinforce my brand. If you are already wandering down the road to brand nowhere then don't despair. It can be fixed. You might have to put aside some things or replicate them under your chosen brand, but it can be done. Try typing Ruby Barnes into Google Search and see if my brand is strong. Try Author Ruby Barnes and it's even deeper.

Components for your platform - overview

Do an inventory of web-based activities that you currently engage in and compare it with this list:

- at least two email addresses, preferably webmail;
- blog and / or website;
- facebook user page, fan page, reader and writer groups;
- twitter membership and twitter related tools such as Hootsuite;
- reader groups e.g. Goodreads, LibraryThing;
- Gravatar;
- other social networks such as Google+, LinkedIn;
- Kindle Direct Publishing;
- Amazon customer and author profiles;
- Smashwords;
- content for all the above.

How did you do? Heard of all of those and already a user? If not, don't worry. There's hand-holding available here in *The New Author*.

You've decided that social media is an essential marketing support for selling your ebook. You recognise that brand and strong product is the key to building market presence and loyal readership. Now it's time to build your platform and interweave the components so they give you maximum brand exposure. Let's look in more detail at how to handle those platform components.

Content - the nitty gritty of your social network platform

Having taken a brief look above at the elements of your social network, the first step is basic content. I have to be honest and say that, of all things, the initial content requirements flummoxed me. After writing 90,000 words I stumbled over short snippets of information about my book and myself. The best advice is to just get on with it. As long as you keep a record of where you place your content, you can always update it later. Okay, let's go.

Who are you? Let's take a look at you and hear where you've come from so we can understand the author behind the book. I want you to go to Amazon top 100 paid kindle books (pull up any kindle book on Amazon kindle store, go to the sales ranking in the product details and click on *See Top 100 Paid in Kindle Store*) then click on any author name that is highlighted blue. You'll see interesting photos and biographies that let you get to know the author. That's what you need to aim for.

Pic - don't be shy and don't use a picture from twenty years ago or some crazy cartoon. Ideally you should have a professionally taken head-and-shoulders smiling pose, but don't get too hung up about that, there are enough other obstacles to overcome. I cut mine from a summer holiday photo and folk seem to like it.

Biography - this is a chance to tell your life story. Every writer I've ever met has an interesting tale of how they got to where they are. Use your own style and let your voice come through. Some people like to talk about themselves in a factual and detached third person manner. Others like to look the reader right between the eyes and let them know what kind of writing awaits them. Have a short and a longer version on hand as there will be occasion for both.

Book cover - remember the book? That's why you're doing all this. You need a front cover for your book, an eye-catching first impression that embodies what your book has to say. Go back to that Amazon kindle top 100 and click on the menu to the left. Open it up until you find your genre. Then scroll down through the thumbnails of the best selling books and get a feel for what catches your eye. With few exceptions, successful ebook covers give a strong image that summarises the feel of the book. They display the title prominently so that it's easily readable in the thumbnail version of the cover that appears on most web stores, and the size of author name increases in proportion to the author's existing brand strength.

Indie ebooks are often immediately identifiable by their homemade covers. There are indie ebooks in the

Amazon US and UK top 100 but you would do well to spot them from the cover. The message is clear – you need a professional looking cover to do justice to the novel you have slaved over. Don't eat the cow and choke on the tail. If you have graphic design expertise then have a go, otherwise find a cover designer through recommendation or from surfing online writing groups. Go armed with example covers that appeal to you from the Amazon top 100 in your genre. Always check a designer's previous work, ensure that they will incorporate subsequent changes within the specified price and, when spending your money, remember that it has to be earned back from sales.

Product description - when you browse a book shop you're going to look at the cover, title and author, and then the back cover blurb. That back cover blurb is what ebook retailers call product description. It's not a synopsis, it's a hook to lure the reader. Again the Amazon top 100 is a good guide to effective, persuasive product description. Pick a book in your genre (if it's from a mainstream publisher you will probably have to click on 'See all Editorial Reviews' because the page will be full of reviews from literary publications).

That product description should leave the potential reader in no doubt about what sort of novel is on offer. Who is the main character, what sort of challenge and choices do they face and how will lives be affected by the outcome? The style of the product description should match your writing voice. A good test of your product description is to show it to someone who has read your novel and ask them if it's representative of the book.

You will need a short and a long version of your product description as some web stores require both. Get it as good as you can before the launch but you'll have opportunities to fine tune as things go along.

Email address - my recommendation is that you have at least two email addresses but redirect all your mails to one inbox. There is going to be a lot of incoming mail but you probably won't be sending a lot of mail out initially.

You might have an email address as part of the package from your internet provider. If not then there are numerous free providers such as Google (gmail) and Microsoft (hotmail). Make sure that any email address you send from has your brand setting i.e. when folk get mail from you it is labelled with your brand, rather than some obscure or humorous name that you devised before you wanted to be a famous author.

Go to your email settings page and enter your brand as your name (usually your author name). You can have more than one email displaying the same brand name.

Why make things so complicated with more than one email address? There are a couple of reasons. Firstly, reliance upon a single email provider is putting all your eggs in one basket. If something goes wrong with that email then you are cut off from the world and, when you're running a social networking platform, being cut off is no fun. Secondly, if you have any multi-administrator components in your platform, such as a blog or facebook fan page, it is a good idea to have more than one administrator login and that means more than one email address.

My personal preference is to use free webmail such as Google or Windows Live / Hotmail. Access is then device independent – useful if you're going to communicate from more than one computer or an internet café etc. Although you can adjust the name that appears on the recipients' screen, do try and choose an email address that looks professional i.e. authorfredblogs@gmail.com rather than something that will give you a chuckle but you may live to regret, such as hotlipsbuffbloke@gmail.com (people can still see your actual email address if they save you to their address book etc.) If your internet provider or website provider gives you an email then you can use that.

Blog or website? - there was a time when a blog was just a plain text diary and a website was a colourful shop front. These days the borders between the two are blurred.

Website - purchasing a URL that matches your brand makes good sense but the design of a professional looking web page can cost a lot of money. It's possible to build a blog into a website but not so easy for a beginner to build into a website the flexibility offered by a dedicated blog. There is an initial temptation to throw money (if you have it) at a website because you want to give a professional impression. That makes sense if you have a backlist of novels and an existing following. If you're new to the game then you will have little idea of what is needed on an author website, not much product to sell and no content to entice viewers. However, if you have decided on a clear brand then the URL for that brand is a valuable commodity, so it's worth checking if your brand URL is available and consider purchasing it. Be careful with this step. Depending upon the route that you buy your URL, it can lead you into a hosting agreement with monthly charges, an awkward design platform or (as happened to me) ownership of a URL that you can't work out how to access.

Blog - there are a number of blog providers that provide free hosting and you can select your brand name, or a variant of it, in the address (if it's available). Blogger (Google) and Wordpress are the two blog providers that are most popular with authors. The design of these blogs is quite easy, with a wide range of standard templates provided, and there are a lot of social networking features and plug-ins (widgets). It's also possible to create additional pages e.g. a shop front. The theoretical disadvantage of free blogs is the provider may make changes, go offline or even close down. This happens rarely but it's always a good idea to keep a backup of the html code of your blog.

Website blog combo - some blog providers offer users the opportunity to purchase (at nominal cost) a branded URL e.g. yourname.com and place your blog at that address.

Website / blog style

The idea of your web presence is to create interest in you as an author. How you do this depends very much upon your personal style. Here are some blogging styles you may recognise after browsing a few websites and blogs.

The Diarist. This is the original blogger, sharing observations of day to day events from the author's life in a diary format. *The Diarist* does have potential to build a cult following but, unless you're in the public eye or live a fascinating life, it's likely to have the readership of a paper diary i.e. just you.

The Writer's Friend. Sharing experiences of your writing journey from inspiration to manuscript completion, working up a social networking platform and publishing an ebook. It can build traffic and followers but, and this is a big but, they will be other writers. That's fine for a how-to book like this one where the target market is new authors, but *The Writer's Friend* isn't of great interest to readers. Friends and colleagues in the writing world can be extremely valuable but, as an author, you also need readers.

The Book Reviewer. Readers are interested in reviews, so this sounds like a no-brainer. Build a blog or website that is jam packed with book reviews. Hyperlink all the reviews to Amazon or another vendor and set up as an affiliate, earning commission on pass-through sales. You won't be the first to do this but it doesn't mean that it's not a business model. What it isn't is promotion of you as an author. If you write entertaining reviews then it is promotion of you as a reviewer. At worst, you will spend all your time reading and reviewing books, neglecting your creative writing. As you become known you will be flooded by independent authors looking to get airtime for their novels. Unless you give everything a glowing review you will inevitably engender some backlash. This isn't the way to go in building your brand. There are successful variations on *The Book Reviewer* – if you stick to your own genre and only review works (indie or mainstream) that you think are 'worthy' then the end result will be positive and it can attract a lot of traffic.

The Storekeeper. Creative writing on a blog or website is too much for some people. They want to write a novel and that's as far as they are prepared to go. So their blog or site is limited to a description of them and their book(s), like a shop display of the product. That's fine and everyone should have this as part of their web presence, but if it's purely a static reference then people will come, take a quick look, move on and probably not come back. If you don't have the appetite for creativity on your blog / site then at least make your content worth more than a passing glance. Include a teaser from your novel and, when you have reviews, post them in their entirety or else post tag lines from those reviews.

The Opinionist. People like to let off steam and / or they like to see others do so. If you have strong opinions on one or more subjects then you might be tempted to share them with the world. If you can do this in a non-offensive, well-written way then it can be a mechanism to pull in web traffic and tune readers to your voice. The risks are obvious. You might alienate potential novel readers with your views, so choose your subjects carefully.

The Serial Offender. Charles Dickens released his novels as instalments. Serials are immensely popular on TV. Surely it makes sense for you to drip feed your reading public with your work, doesn't it? The jury is out on novelists putting their work up on the web in instalments. It will probably only work if you are already well known and your site has existing traffic.

There are downsides to *The Serial Offender* approach. The instalments need to work as standalone pieces otherwise someone who wanders onto your blog will feel disorientated, like they walked into a film, part way through. Another pitfall is that, if you post on a regular basis, you will soon be giving away a substantial portion of your novel for free. Why then should a reader buy your book if they can simply wait for the next chapter on the blog?

The Entertainer. This style is something like a newspaper columnist. They write short articles on whatever subject comes to mind. It might be a true story, commentary on current affairs, a piece of flash fiction or a personal or industry news item. If *The Entertainer* has an appealing and characteristic style of writing then the blog can become an ezine of sorts. Regular readers are likely to be attracted to the author's style and, if they read books, may well buy the blogger's novel. The risk here is you might write a very good novel but not be good at short pieces of entertainment. *The Entertainer* is the default style that springs to mind when someone says they are a blogger, but very few can actually entertain.

The Hobbyist. You might consider writing to be your hobby (or maybe you consider writing to be your life and that demon day job to be a money hobby). Some people have serious hobbies they are very passionate about and they choose to blog on topic. It might be gardening, collecting mountain crystals, dinosaur hunting, playing bluegrass guitar or anything. The blog, if well written, will be of interest to other hobbyists of that persuasion. But will someone buy your crime thriller novel because you share an interest in cross-breeding roses? They might consider your writing to be another, less important hobby than your horticultural interests.

The Professional. This is a perverse variant on *The Hobbyist. The Professional's* blog or web page content is dedicated to whatever the blogger does for a day job. This might be something arty like 18th century knitwear or something technical like astrophysics. The author's novel is added on as an afterthought and the effect is to put a definite hobby emphasis on the book. It may be that people interested in 18th century knitwear are desperate to read an historical novel featuring characters clad in the aforementioned clothing. That could work, although the knitwear may not work as a great initial blog hook and will probably funnel a very limited readership. However, if the novel is science fiction or a crime thriller then you might lose the knitwear fan along the way. The main downfall of both *The*

Professional and *The Hobbyist* is that potential readers trafficking through your blog will very likely have a 'huh?' moment when they hit the hobby or professional content. If you are determined to have an internet presence for your day job or hobby then it's best to keep it separate and outside your author social network platform (of course a link here or there is okay).

The Visual Artist. Line after line of print in blog posts can be monotonous. So why not brighten it up with pictures that reinforce the points you are trying to make? Go grab some public domain images from somewhere. Add some colour, give it a mood, visualise. The result can be very pretty to look at but, again, there are downfalls.

I had one writer friend compliment me on the variety of pictures I was using in one of my posts at the time. The viewing figures were very high and we both attributed that to the content and presentation. It took me several months to realise that viewers were finding my blog by following search engine links to pictures of elephants. In fact, half of my viewers were looking for elephants, staying just a few seconds and then heading off again (more about analytics later). I thought a ton of folk were looking at my stuff but it was the pachyderms that were pulling them in. Goes to show that Google image search is very effective!

Another pitfall of images is that they can take a long time to load and view, or might not view well or at all on mobile devices. Regardless of your blog style, it's always worth checking out how your blog presents on different devices and in different browsers.

In conclusion, if you're not sure which style will suit you and your potential readership then take your time, experiment and see what works. You can always delete posts if you deem them a failure. My own blog is a mixture of *Entertainer, Book Reviewer, Writer's Friend* and *Shopkeeper*. I post the mixture on my home page and siphon it off to separate pages for reviews, shop, and writing advice. This gives me the opportunity to post different links for different audiences on various places in my platform.

Must-haves for your blog / webpage

Once you choose your blog or web provider, follow their tutorial on how to set up your page. There are numerous standard templates to choose from and the layout is easy to customise with a wide range of standard add-ons provided. You can also grab plug-ins as html code from all kinds of sources on the web and embed them in the design of your page by switching the design view to html. Usual software download precautions apply regarding trusting the supplier of widgets and code. This might sound like gobbledegook to you here and now, but the online tutorial of your provider will make sense of it.

There are some key components that you should consider for your web presence. The objective is to attract and retain viewers, ideally re-routing them to a place of purchase for your novel.

A clear title and description

It should be obvious to the visitor that they have landed on the blog of [Brand Name] who is an author of [Genre Novels]. You should also add any other blogging style that you use e.g. ebook author, reviewer and blogger. Apart from the visual impact, these titles will be the main features of your blog to be picked up by search engines.

Views counter

You might not want to install this immediately but, when you begin to gain good traffic on your blog, it can be a good idea to show its popularity.

Ways to connect

There are a number of ways for a surfer to index a blog of interest, in addition to the traditional marking as a favourite, and the most common ones are listed below.

Follow on twitter

Opens a new window where the visitor can follow you on twitter, providing they have a twitter account. You can get various widgets on the internet that also show your number of twitter followers and even your latest tweets.

Follow with login

Google Blogger and Wordpress automatically give follow options at the top of the blog but the followers must be a registered Google or Wordpress user. Blogger also has a 'Join this site with Google Friend Connect' widget that you can plug into your blog design, displaying the number and pictures of followers.

Follow with Networked Blogs

A web app that gives you feeds from blogs that you follow and allows you to connect to other blogs.

Follow by email

The reader will enter their email address and subscribe to your blog. Whenever there are new posts they will receive an email carrying a truncated version (or you can set to full version) of that new post. Note: this isn't a mail list but an automatic subscription.

Follow by RSS

Some people prefer to receive RSS feeds of new blog items. They view their RSS feeds in a browser or dashboard and can see when something new comes along.

Subscribe to updates

This is a place where followers enter their email address for addition to your mail list. They don't receive any updates until you decide to send something manually or by using an email package such as MailChimp.

Like on facebook

A widget that will add the visitor to the list of people who like your facebook fan page, providing they have a facebook account. There are variants on this that will take the visitor to your facebook fan or author page, or simply put a 'like' notice on their facebook newsfeed for others to see.

Your novel

Don't be shy about showing your book on your blog or web page. It's a good idea not to shout that the web page is all about your book, unless you just want it to be a shop front (which is okay if that's your chosen style). Do let the viewers catch a glimpse of your cover and be sure to give a buy link or hyperlink the cover image to your preferred place of purchase or book detail page.

Blogroll

As you come across other blogs of interest, you might want to share them with your own visitors. These should be blogs that you personally recommend and, by linking to them, you can often agree a link back from the target blog to yours, increasing potential traffic.

Search Engine Optimisation SEO for your blog / website

You've decided on your blog style, layout and content. Now you need to make sure that you're getting found on Google, Bing, Yahoo and other search engines. SEO is the method of making your web presence easily found through giving it a high profile in search engines. Try typing *Peril by Ruby Barnes* into a search engine and scroll through the results. All the ebook marketplaces feature strongly in those results as they are designed in a way that promotes their products through SEO. I'm a self-confessed non-expert in SEO but there are some basic things you can do to optimise your search results. If you already know about SEO, html and meta tags then look away now! What follows is for beginners, which is the place I started from.

Your blog has a number of key places where search engines will index it against keywords. Some people may dispute this, but I know it's correct because I've tested it with improbable search words.

Title

Your actual on-page blog title is the main key to visibility. Include your brand and what you do e.g. *Ruby Barnes ebook author*. The blog will automatically embed your actual page title in the html code of your page and, within a few days, it will be found by search engine spider bots and indexed so that you come up in searches. If you're determined to label your blog page with something other than your brand then the branded URL will still come up in search but not as the first line.

HTML

The automatic placement of your blog title in the html code can be further exploited. Go to the design page of your blog and click on edit html. After the code *<head>* you will see your blog title e.g. *<title>Ruby Barnes - ebook author, book reviewer, blogger</title>*. Note that this contains the words *book reviewer, blogger* which don't appear in my on-page title, but they do appear in the search engine result for my blog. This shows that you can have terms appear in the search engine that don't have to appear on the blog page.

I also have the words *Ruby Barnes writes thrillers, reviews books, sells ebooks and advises on novel writing, social media and ebook publication* bounded by the code *<meta content=* and *name='description'/>*. Those words appear on the third line of the search engine result although they don't appear on my blog page.

So the search engine result looks like this:

Ruby Barnes - ebook author, book reviewer, blogger

rubybarnes.blogspot.com/

14 Jan 2012 – Ruby Barnes writes thrillers, reviews books, sells ebooks and advises on novel writing, social media and ebook publication.

The only words that are on the page are *Ruby Barnes –ebook author*. The rest are meta tags embedded in the html code.

That's just the baby steps but it's that easy. Except maybe you've chosen wording that no one is searching for. That's another matter. One way SEO companies provide value is in their knowledge of which search terms will get results and whereabouts on your platform you should place those terms. There are seemingly limitless resources on the web for SEO. Type SEO Analyzer (yes, US spelling for a change) into Google and you will find various free tools that will analyse your web page from a search engine perspective. There are also lots of free SEO guides available on the web that will take you deeper into the art if you really want to go there.

Tags on your blog posts

When you've created a piece of content for your blog, don't forget to add some suitable tags to it. Choose words that you would enter into a search engine if you wanted to find a post like the one you have written.

Text content of your blog posts

Search engines will also pick up words and phrases from your blog posts. Bear that in mind when blogging. Don't miss a chance to mention your book or other authors. Try and use memorable hooks for your blog titles and closing sentences. For example, try typing *tired old limes stand the test of time* into Google. It's the title of a post I wrote reviewing *The Green Mile* by Stephen King. You'll see that the first two results are my blog and the next are places where my blog is syndicated to (more about syndication later).

Blog comments

Once you have attracted an audience to your blog, let those who are not too shy make a comment if they wish. Enable comments on your posts in the blog settings. It might take a while for people to pluck up the courage to post a comment, unless you write a particularly controversial blog post. When someone does comment then make sure to respond with a comment of your own and do it in an appreciative and chatty fashion so that others will be encouraged to comment on that post or others.

Don't handle comments like a lecturer or politician taking questions. You want to engender discussion, make people feel like they should come back regularly, and solicit further comment from new visitors. If you get an abusive comment then you, as blog owner, can always delete it.

If you don't get any comments on your blog then it may be for a number of reasons. Perhaps your blog traffic isn't really there to read your posts (like the elephant hunters I mentioned above). Maybe you didn't solicit comment with the style of your post. It could also be that you're appearing too needy e.g. *Please, please let me know what you think!* Unless you are using the post to solicit opinion, such as which draft of your book's front cover is the best, it's often best to imply a question rather than ask it outright. The other day I saw a blog post ranting about the fact that no one had commented on the previous post that had ended *What do you think?* No one commented on the rant either.

Captcha and moderation

Most blogs offer a Captcha option which requires the reader to interpret a slightly confused set of letters and enter them into a submit box. The idea is to prove that the reader is human and not a bot, thereby avoiding spam comments. I don't like to use Captcha because I want it to be as easy as possible for readers to post comments on my blog. Similarly, I don't use the moderation option where the blog owner has to approve comments before they get posted on the blog. Apart from free speech arguments, it interrupts spontaneity if a conversation develops in the comments section. On the other hand, I've been lucky in that I haven't had any crazed stalkers or spam-posting bots on my blog (at time of writing).

There's usually a spam section in the blog dashboard and you should check that regularly in case some valid comments have been parked there by the blog spam filter.

Blog pages

Many blogs only use a single front page but most blog providers let you set up additional pages so that the effect is like a website. If you have a lot of content right from the get go e.g. blog posts, teasers from your book, a mail list form or contact page, a shop front, then you might like to start off with several pages. Otherwise let it evolve but keep an eye on the developing mix of content you have and solicit feedback from viewers about whether they enjoy your blog experience and if the page loads fast enough. As you build traffic and content there may come a time to separate your blog into pages for different content types. That will help you point visitors in the right direction for their needs e.g. people who are interested in book reviews at one page, fellow authors who want to read about your trials and tribulations at another page, and straightforward book buyers into your online shop.

Leverage all your blog content, old and new

If you manage to maintain a high quality of blog post then you can continue to reap the benefit of your efforts as time goes on. As long as you leave the blog settings so each new post has a unique URL, you can link to the post in other social media when an audience presents itself. For example, if you write a post about your success or otherwise with query letters then you can periodically mention it on twitter as you gather new followers, or refer to it in writer forum discussions on that topic.

Blog analytics

At time of writing my blog page views have just passed 23,000. There was a time when I thought nobody was ever going to read my blog. Then I wrote a post about Compulsive Communication Syndrome (which isn't a clinical condition, I made it up). The number of views on my blog increased dramatically. However, after a few weeks of feeling like I had actually written something that people from around the world were interested in, it came to light that 75% of my visitors were looking for pictures of elephants. Their average stay was just over 2 seconds. I had used a picture of elephants and an elephant joke in my post. Therein lies a lesson – a lot of people like elephants. If you can leverage your blog content to match topic popularity with the top interests of your potential readers then the traffic volume becomes much more meaningful.

The next breakthrough was when I took a family holiday and had to survive without internet for a week. I had started using a twitter tool called Hootsuite (more on that later) and what I did was to pre-schedule tweets during that week, pointing to blog posts that I had written in the previous months. The result was more than one hundred hits per day, every day, but half of them were still short-stay elephant hunters.

I was enjoying the blog traffic (a pointless obsession with numbers) but really wanted to up the quantity of hits from genuinely interested readers and writers. So I started to research SEO on the internet, made some changes, ran my pages through an SEO analyzer and tuned things up a bit. I managed to get a mention on the Smashwords blog and more traffic came to my blog from there.

The result is that my blog traffic is now predominantly viewing my posts rather than searching for elephant pictures. Visitors stay minutes rather than seconds and sometimes for more than an hour, moving from post to post and page to page. I get a feeling for whether folks are looking at my shop, either of my two book pages, my New Author post, the shop or the main blog page.

The reason I shared this little insight of blog statistics is that analytics are important. There are basic analytics built into most blog platforms that tell you the total number of views per post and page, the traffic sources (including referring URLs, referring sites and search keywords) and the geographical audience. You can set up your blog for deeper information through tools such as Google Analytics to gain a more in-depth understanding. Know your audience.

Facebook

Before I got started with all this social network platform carry-on, friends and family used to tell me that I should be on facebook. So I took a look but couldn't understand what all the fuss was about. It wasn't that I was a technophobe - my day job involved a fair amount of technology including global conferences with chat and video. I just couldn't see a place in my life for facebook. One day a writing course colleagues in Kilkenny pinned me to a chair, thrust her laptop at me and forced me to create a facebook page which then sat dormant for twenty-four months.

The seasons came and went. Then a new dawn of independent ebook publishing broke and I got out my surf board to ride the wave. Social media gurus advocated using MySpace, LinkedIn, facebook and other social networks to build an author platform. I was already using LinkedIn for my day job persona, so that one was off the list (my writer persona has just recently started with LinkedIn). MySpace seemed to take forever to load and I soon discovered that there had been some sort of melt-down and a general migration to facebook. So I focused on facebook and proceeded to make a bucketful of mistakes. Let's look and learn from what I did.

The main email that I use for funnelling correspondence didn't seem to be accepted by facebook. It said that somebody was already using that email. I was outraged. Identity theft! Determined to hack into the imposter's account, I entered password after password and eventually managed to log in with a made up word that no one else could possibly know. What did I find? A user with the name of one of my novel characters, Ger Mayes, and a black and white profile picture of me looking overweight with a very bad haircut. There were comments on the profile picture. I read them and it all came back to me. This had been my facebook persona for the past two years, foisted upon me by my Kilkenny writing friends. So I updated the photo and offered friendship to a few mutual friends, the social circle peaking at about twelve (I have a very small circle of friends in real life). It was fun to play the role of anti-hero Ger Mayes, he's such a loser.

The next mistake I made was to create a facebook account with a picture of a turnip as the avatar and the username of, wait for it, Turnip. I had been active in online writing groups under that name and enjoyed making vegetable-based jokes. It sounds ridiculous, but it was more ridiculous than it sounds. There was really no way that anyone could find me by my real name or pen name. I friended all the online writers that I knew, some of Ger Mayes' friends too, and that social circle grew to around twenty-five people.

Mistake three was to let the main character of my next novel get in on the act. John Baptist, the serial killer, friended just those who knew his story and he spoke to them strictly in character.

The total folly of this became apparent to me one weekend when, the entire family being away in Dublin, I had three laptops open and all three characters logged in to a chat group. After a very confusing hour of chatting with others in my three roles, and sometimes between my selves, someone asked where Ruby Barnes was. A little bell rang in the heads of all three of me and I sacked them, each and every one. It was brand confusion on a cosmic scale.

In my defence, I was just starting out and the chaos only lasted for a few weeks. Ger Mayes became Ruby Barnes and all existing friends were informed of that. I began to offer friendship to friends of friends that I knew would be involved in writing, wherever possible sending them a message to explain who I was and why I was offering friendship. Almost everyone accepted. Ruby's circle of friends grew from twenty-five to fifty. Around that point people started to offer me friendship. The number of friends grew to one hundred.

A word of caution. It is important to build your social network but take care not to be seen as an annoyance or a source of spam. Some people on facebook treat the friends concept as they do in real life. They only want interaction with people they know personally. If you add someone as a friend and a message pops up on your screen that you should only friend them if you really know them, then take it seriously. In a frenzy to gather virtual friends for your network you might be reported as a spammer and banned from facebook for a couple of days, a month or forever.

Make sure that the people you friend are treating facebook as a virtual network. A good indication of this is if they share a number of mutual friends with you.

Facebook as a 'username'

This is the normal type of facebook page and is intended for individuals. You have a 'wall' where you can post status updates, photos and links that will appear in the newsfeed of people who are on your friend list. People recognise you by your name and avatar, and you have an info page for those that want to know more. You can post on other people's walls, send them private messages or hold an online chat. As a user you can join facebook groups that are oriented around a particular interest and join in the discussions on the group wall. Groups are also a good place to find new like-minded friends. The possibilities are extensive but be aware that as your number of facebook friends grows and the number of groups you join increases, the resulting traffic can become overwhelming. It can absorb your time.

People who are using facebook as part of a social network platform often use their name page as a brand page. They might use their latest book cover as an avatar and feed their wall with continuous promotion material. The limit on number of friends that an individual can have on facebook is 5,000 and those type of brand pages usually have around that number of friends. Above 5,000 friends the owner of the page will be pushed towards using a fan page.

My preference is to operate on facebook with my user name, my facebook friends consisting mostly of other authors. I find it to be a very supportive community when used that way and have built a network of over 700 people.

Facebook as a 'page'

Since facebook introduced the 5,000 friend limit for individual users, it's been necessary to create a 'page' if you want to hold a larger audience. The page facility isn't as flexible as the username. Your page persona or brand can't join groups and doesn't have the same messaging and friending capabilities as your username. It tends to be used as a facebook viewing window on general news posts and many platform owners auto-syndicate their blog posts to it. If you plan to post general news to your username wall then the brand page content should be something different e.g. product, your novels.

Facebook groups

Facebook has more than 845 million active users (at time of writing) with 152 million in the US alone. Not all of them are potential readers of your book but many surely are. Most people that I know have no more than a few hundred friends on facebook but they interact with a larger number of folk via facebook interest groups. Some groups are just a few tens of people and others run into thousands. The groups may be open access, private and by invitation or request only, or actually really a brand page that allows discussion. One or more moderators will administer the group, outline the areas for discussion and activity, set the ground rules and, if necessary, police the proceedings.

At last count I am a member of 17 facebook groups ranging in size from 10 to 1006 members. Half of these groups are author only and the other half are a mixture of readers and authors. Facebook groups can be very beneficial but they can also be time-consuming and frustrating. Here are some suggestions to help you with getting the most out of them.

- First decide what your objectives are and search for a group that looks like it can further your objectives. Use the facebook search box or ask facebook friends for recommendations.

- When you find a likely group, look at the number of members, whether the group is open or closed, and check out their wall or docs for their charter, statement of purpose or similar. If it still matches your needs then go about joining the group, using an introduction by your contact in the case of a closed group.

- **Change the *Notifications* settings for the group immediately after joining**, otherwise your email will be flooded with notifications of group activity. If it's a large and industrious group then this can be an overwhelming volume.

- Tread carefully in the group and find your way around what the group protocol is, making sure to read and digest reference documents etc.

- The group charter is likely to place constraints upon marketing within the group by members. Example: *this independent author group is a place for indie authors and readers to interact and to help each other with suggestions, tips, marketing, reviews, etc. It is not an opportunity to market your books/services. The mission is to assist members of the group in becoming better writers.*

- If you blast the group with a hit and run of your novel details every time you post then they will likely throw you out. But if you become an active member of the group they will support you in your marketing efforts on your platform e.g. how best to use twitter and how to set up a circle of friends to retweet book marketing info, how to get likes for your facebook page, how to get your books tagged and how to grow the number of followers of your platform components.

Group members will likely accept your offer of facebook friendship but many will first want to see that you fit into the group way of working and aren't going to spam them. This is especially true if it's a group that included readers. Their support has to be earned whereas the friendship of other authors can often be acquired through an expectation of mutual support.

Independent authors often forget that, in order to succeed, they need to develop a loyal readership beyond the boundaries of other independent authors.

Indie authors do buy and read books but just selling to each other isn't a long-term strategy. It's more of a pyramid strategy. Like Goodreads, LibraryThing and other networks, facebook has millions of potential readers for your work. Always remember that your objective is to use your platform to hook those readers.

Twitter

I have never been a fan of text or short messages. When I heard that there was this thing called twitter and that a posh UK comedian named Stephen Fry was 'tweeting' short status messages to thousands of followers about being stuck in a lift, I thought the world had gone mad. Millions of people compulsively throwing 140 character obscure, mundane, banal compositions into the ether, every second of the day. What could possibly be the point of it?

At time of writing I have a modest twitter following of 2,250 people, a mixture of readers and authors. I have sold books to followers, picked up endless tips on writing, social networking and epublishing, and made some genuine friends with whom I chat on twitter. I can reuse all my successful blog posts on a scheduled basis so that new followers have a chance to read all I have to offer, and each tweet drives a certain amount of traffic to my blog. And sometimes, just sometimes, I plug my novels. So, how did I manage the transition from doubter to believer? Let's consider.

Twitter Step 1 - brand identification

Your name and image should be your brand. In the great maelstrom that is twitter, this is extremely important. You will get recognition on twitter for your avatar, your name and your content. If I call myself Turnip then that doesn't help my Ruby Barnes brand. People might like my tweet content but they won't associate it with Ruby Barnes. If I use a sexy avatar then I will get all the wrong kinds of people following me. Using my regular avatar (hey, who says it isn't sexy? Okay, the truth hurts) will let people know it's the same Ruby Barnes silver fox guy that runs that blog, writes those novels and interacts in online groups about reading and writing.

Everything that you do on twitter is in the name of your brand, so stay aware of that if you engage directly with people on twitter. Courteous, entertaining, confident, authorly (made-up word), that's how we need to comport (not a made-up word) ourselves.

Twitter Step 2 - learning the twitter ropes

Twitter might be a fairly intuitive environment for those who live by mobile text messages, but there's a steep learning curve for most of us. When you sign up for twitter there is a brief online tutorial that might help, and I suggest you follow it. You can buy how-to books devoted to twitter usage but I've outlined the key beginner's points below.

Tweets - when you write out your message (140 characters max.) and send, it is immediately in the public domain. It joins the continuous flurry of tweets from any one of up to 300 million global twitter users and your tweet content is searchable by word content (and username, but nobody knows you exist yet).

Following - as you start to follow people, their tweets will appear in your timeline, which is your newsfeed. Twitter encourages new members to follow some celebrities as a starting point. If you are already involved in author or reader groups on facebook or Goodreads etc, then it is probably a better idea to tell members that you're starting with twitter and then begin following some group members. These groups often have a chat thread where they share their twitter user names and it's easy to follow them. You'll see from their tweets how they use twitter. Or you can follow me @Ruby_Barnes. My twitter stream, for example, is a mix of top of the head nonsense that makes me run to the computer and type, links and lines to my historic blog posts, news of new reviews for my books, and retweets of other folks' stuff.

Reply - if you see something in your feed that you want to respond to then click on it and then hit reply. Your message box will have @ plus their username in it. Prefixing a tweet with @ and someone's twitter name is a way of chatting in public, so make sure it's something that you don't mind other folk seeing. They might join in the chat.

Direct message – sending a message is private between you and the recipient. If you click the envelope symbol then the message box will appear. Another way to do this is to prefix your correspondent's username with *d* and a space (direct message). You can only direct message someone who is already following you.

Hashtags # - as your timeline becomes busier you'll see people including hashtags in their tweets. This is an attempt to engage in global conversations on the topic that hashtag describes or to attract the attention of twitter users that might search for that hashtag. Phrases or hashtags that have a lot of people following them are called trends and you can see the top trends on the right of your Home page. At time of writing, #LastTimeIChecked was the top global trend and people were sharing all kinds of serious and less serious insights into their lives. If you see a trend that is somehow relevant to your target audience then you might try friending some participants.

New followers, follow-back and bots – it can be quite exhilarating to get new followers, especially if it seems to be in response to your tweets. It's considered courteous to follow-back all your new followers, having first checked their profile to ensure that they're someone you want to interact with. There are bots that snap up hundreds of followers based upon word searches and other criteria, but you can recognise them from the small number of nonsensical tweets on their timeline. I often respond to new followers with a thank-you @ mention or direct message, offering them to go take a look at my blog. I've never had anyone complain about that, it helps blog traffic and individuals have thanked me for the personalised message. As your number of followers increases it can be too time-consuming to keep this up.

Spam and viruses – if you receive a mention or direct message from anyone, even a friend / follower, that looks something like *Wow! You should see what terrible things this person is saying about you! http://tinyurl.123abc* then never, ever click on the link. Delete immediately or check with the sender that it's genuine. These are virus messages that will hijack your twitter account and send similar messages from you to your followers without your knowledge. If you do get caught then immediately log out of twitter, log back in and change your password.

If you get a number of new followers that seem to have a wide network but very few tweets, and even the same tweets as each other, then these are likely to be spam bots. There's no point in trying to correspond with the spam bots but you can block the user or report them for spam.

Tweet privacy and follower validation - some people don't want their tweets to be public domain but only visible to followers, and those followers have to be individually approved by the user. That's fine for a closed circle of friends but not suitable for the social network platform that you need to build as it constrains organic growth of your network, so make sure this option is unchecked on your twitter settings. Another facility used by some is the TrueTwit validation service. This requires a follower to go to a third party website and enter a captcha code or adjust a rotatable graphic before they are allowed to follow you. The idea is that spam and malicious bots will be thwarted from following. If you really want every new follower to have to go through this process then do so but it will deter some genuine followers and can cause delays in building your network, so I recommend against it. It's easy enough to spot and block the bots.

Twitter Step 3 - Developing your content and building the network

Writing tweets of 140 characters is extreme flash fiction. In fact, you have less than 140 characters if you are sending an @ or d message as the @ or d and username eat into the 140. Also, if you want people to be able to easily retweet (RT) your tweet then you need to stop short of the 140 by however many characters are in 'RT @yourusername', otherwise your carefully crafted message may be truncated by the RT 140 limit.

When writing your tweet consider carefully exactly what you want to say and who your audience is. A jokey one liner is easy enough. If it's snappy when delivered verbally then it'll work as a tweet. Attempting to drive traffic to your blog, your book page or somewhere else is more tricky. You need a hook to grab the attention of passing eyes as they scan the myriad tweets rolling down their timeline. The best approach is trial and error. Hashtags can also come into play but they require you to second guess which if any hashtags or keywords your target audience might be searching for.

Consider these two marketing tweets:

Please buy my new ebook The Baptist by Ruby Barnes, a psychological thriller on http://www.amazon.com/The-Baptist-ebook/dp/B006112NO8 (133 characters)

versus

The Baptist by Ruby Barnes ebook http://ow.ly/8f3g6 All chiller, no filler #thriller #serialkiller Pls RT (105 characters)

Of these two messages, the second picks up a lot more responses. It's more snappy, stylised (that's a risk, I know), uses hashtags for anyone searching those terms, is short for easy RT and even requests RTs. The link, rather than an Amazon product page, actually goes to the blog where the book is introduced and existing reader reviews can be seen.

Here's another example:

New blog post about profanity in The Baptist by Ruby Barnes http://rubybarnes.blogspot.com/2011/12/profane-language-dont-read-on.html (134 characters)

versus

WTF? Spam filter intercepts The Baptist by Ruby Barnes for profane language! ow.ly/7NGNn (89 characters)

Again the second tweet is crisper, more interesting and generated a lot of traffic to the blog post.

Links in tweets - you can see from the above examples that there are ways of abbreviating URLs to use less of the 140 character limit. Twitter will automatically abbreviate any links to 19 characters but you can get shorter links by using other approaches. The above Baptist blog post link is 73 characters long. Twitter will shorten that to 19. Tinyurl.com will shorten it to 26 and Hootsuite (see below) will shorten it to 11. Shortened links obviously save you tweet character space but they do look anonymous and people may be reluctant to click on them. It's important that the text in the tweet gives readers a clear and inviting message so that they will click.

RT Retweets – one of the beauties of twitter is that your potential reach is multiplied by the number of followers that each person who follows you has. If you have fifty followers, and they each have one hundred followers, then potentially your tweet can reach the timeline of 50 x 100 = 5000 people (or *tweeps* - much as I hate that word, had to use it in the end). To reach your followers' followers, they must retweet (RT) what you have written.

RT can be a very powerful tool but, unless you have written something priceless, you won't get a lot of RTs without first building a relationship with your followers. There are a number of ways to do that. You can work in a pack with friends from e.g. a facebook writers' group and RT each other (as long as you don't all share the same followers, otherwise it's pointless). You can RT other people's tweets of interest and leverage that for reciprocation. You can study your followers, RTs, and statistics on your blog or elsewhere to identify which followers seem to be influencers and then build an ongoing, mutually beneficial twitter relationship with them.

At this point I can recommend Kristen Lamb's book *We Are Not Alone: The Writer's Guide to Social Media*. It contains extensive suggestions on how to categorise your tweeps according to their network influence and how to leverage your network.

Using RT should be done with consideration of your audience. If your stream of tweets becomes a mass push for books of friends then you may lose followers if they feel that they're being spammed with ads. You should RT messages that you think will be of interest to your followers, but check out the message link first. Your RT, your reputation.

Syndication – one of the great things about a social network platform is that you can echo your words of wisdom around the twittersphere, blogosphere, facebook etc. For example, my Ruby Barnes author page on Amazon shows the latest tweet by Ruby_Barnes. Sometimes, when I look at what pops up there, it reminds me of the broader audience that I've syndicated my tweets to. Worth bearing in mind when I tweet a rude joke. You can also flash over new blog posts or other things of interest direct to your twitter account, but copy pasting a link and writing your own tagline is often more effective.

Handling the following / follower balance – some people only want a handful of followers that they will interact with on a controlled basis. Others want to achieve fame or notoriety and gather a million followers like some kind of celebrity. As an independent ebook author using a social platform to reinforce your brand, you should aim somewhere in the middle. The more good quality followers you have, the bigger your immediate brand audience. The more high quality referrer followers you have, the broader your reach.

One strategy would be to only look for high quality referrers as followers, but that's easier said than done. Until you have a critical mass of followers and a respectable number of tweets in your history, you may struggle to attract new followers or gain 100% follow-back.

Building up your network needs to be done in a controlled manner. The first 50 or 100 followers will be hard work. Don't obsess on the numbers too much or overly fret when someone unfollows you. Try to keep the number that you are following not too distant from your number of followers. You don't want to appear too needy. Use tools such as *who.unfollowed.me* to check who has unfollowed you and who isn't following back. It's easy to accidentally unfollow somebody with a stray click of the mouse. If a friend or colleague unfollows then send them an @ message saying *hey, follow me*. Every week or so, after a couple of days of not following anyone new, check who isn't following you back and consider dropping them from your follow list. Some people have such a strong brand that they don't need to follow-back or they are testing their brand strength by suddenly dropping nearly all of their followers. If you're more interested in what their brand has to say than the likelihood of them doing an RT for you, then keep them. If not, unfollow.

Every day or two, follow another 10 or so new tweeps who look like they follow-back. You can judge this from their ratio of following to followers. Give them time to follow back. If you're in an authors' or readers' group that shares twitter details then whack them all in. Then, once a week, cull those that haven't followed back. They might not have had time to pick up your interest but if they do subsequently follow you then you can just follow them back.

Once your followers reach around 100 you will start to get followed by people you don't know. I get followed by between 5 and 20 new people a day. If they look like readers or authors, if their timeline contains sensible content and if their number following isn't too far ahead of their followers then I'll follow-back.

Hope you followed all that! My F key is wearing out.

Advanced twitter-based programmes – it won't be long until the number of tweets in your timeline runs down the page like screen credits too small and fast to read. You'll come back to your twitter page after several hours of some diversionary activity (like sleep or creative writing) and find that so much has been written by so many that you can't keep on top of it. Also it'll become apparent there are bursts of activity in different time zones and you'll have missed the opportunity to address those tweeps. At this point you'll be ready to give up on twitter as a pile of nonsense. The solution is to migrate to a different way of viewing and using twitter with a third party programme.

If you click on any tweet in your timeline you will see the full tweet appear on the right and underneath it the elapsed time and the source, designated by the word *via*. This source is often something other than *web*. Here are just a few from my timeline: Hootsuite, Meltwater Buzz, SocialOomph, Triberr, TweetDeck, twitterfeed. These twitter-focused platforms provide features such as setting up timeline columns that stream tweets according to your criteria e.g. a column each for home feed, mentions, direct messages, sent tweets, my tweets retweeted, scheduled tweets, search by book name, favourite hashtags etc.

Another advantage of some of these advanced twitter interfaces is the ability to schedule tweets. Using this function you can reach out to followers in very different time zones to yours, experimenting with the same tweet at different times of day. My time zone is London GMT and followers respond well from about 11 a.m. onwards but I can also get good global response to scheduled tweets up to 5 a.m., giving increased traffic to the blog and ebooks.

Over the course of time you will discover which style of tweet produces the results you're looking for, be it more followers, retweets, increased blog traffic through links, straight book sales or just your own entertainment. Keep an electronic list of your best tweets (I use an excel spreadsheet for mine) so that you can reuse them periodically. This works especially well for those blog posts that you slaved over months ago. All your good content retains potential value (unless it's seasonal or current affairs related) and new followers won't have seen your older material, so continue to share and benefit. If you're going to be away from your computer for a while then you can schedule a number of interesting daily tweets to go out in your absence, making sure to keep the repetition rate low.

Reader groups

A huge reading public is out there and waiting for your novel. As an independent author the challenge is for you to get your brand and your books in front of that reading public. Many readers are not yet tuned in to ebooks but these days very few people are unable to operate a computer or smartphone. Broadband internet access is a prerequisite for children's homework and an increasing amount of day-to-day domestic administration is carried out on the web. Your brand needs to be in front of as many potential readers as possible and that's why a presence in large marketplaces such as Amazon is a good idea for independent authors.

Most folk read but some folk really consume books, both ebooks and paper books. Enthusiastic readers gather together in reading groups and swoop down upon bookshops to buy ten copies of that month's read. However, physical reading groups aren't everyone's cup of tea and increasing numbers of avid readers are turning to the internet for companionship. According to Wikipedia the predominant English language online reader organisations or *social cataloguing websites* are Goodreads, LibraryThing, Shelfari, aNobii and weRead. There are many others too. I'm going to talk you through Goodreads.

Goodreads

Goodreads is the world's largest English language social cataloguing website and it started up in 2006. Member numbers have mushroomed to over 6.9 million with over 240 million books added to member libraries (there will be duplication in that 240 million, obviously more than one person has stacked the same book on their virtual shelves). The site, in common with other social cataloguing sites, provides some great facilities for readers. They can read member reviews, explore books by genre or author, write their own reviews, engage in discussion groups, network with other readers and even gain direct access to authors who participate in the website. And that's going to be you; an author who participates in the website. At time of writing there are 35,641 authors on Goodreads. This reader and author community is a huge resource.

Some independent authors are intimidated by Goodreads, based upon their experiences there. They consider it a harsh environment for authors. As a reader and an author I consider it to be a very healthy environment. It's a place for me to list 145 books that I've read and post 38 reviews, mostly of those that I've enjoyed, but a few critical reviews too. I mainly review mainstream published books. That gives me some credibility as a reader on Goodreads and shows that I understand what makes a book work or not work for me.

Goodreads is also a place for me to interact with some of the 50,000+ groups that are set up by members for authors, readers or mixed. In the latter two types of groups I interact primarily as a reader, unless the group has a section for authors, in which case I strut my stuff appropriately there. In the author groups it's okay to give your author persona more of a free rein and there are strong learning benefits to be had such as advice on all aspects of writing, promotion and networking.

Most author groups have discussion threads which share twitter, blog and facebook details of members and they can be invaluable for building the author component of your social network. In all cases the same guidelines apply as with facebook groups - tread carefully in the group and find your way around what the group protocol is, making sure to read and digest reference documents etc. Make your introductions, thank the moderator and set out your stall in a relaxed and appropriate manner that suggests you are there to stay.

If you do a hit and run with a book promo then you risk not only being alienated from the group but also marginalising yourself from the huge readership that is Goodreads. Remember, this website has as many reviews per title as Amazon and sometimes more. Goodreads members are the vocal tip of the global English-reading iceberg.

Here are the suggested steps for your expedition into Goodreads (if you're not already a member). Note that it may take a few days or even a week or two for you to complete all this:

- Take a piece of paper and a pen and go write down the title and author of all the books in your house, or as many as you can before your hand gets sore (because who writes with a pen or pencil these days?) Don't worry if you have read those books or not. Include any ebooks you have on a kindle, nook, laptop or wherever.

- Sign up for a Goodreads account and add all the books on your list to your account. This will take some time but the idea is that you show your library to other members. If you have written any book reviews then dig them out and post them on your Goodreads books, together with a score out of five. If you don't have a review for a book but have a strong recollection of your opinion after reading, then just give a score out of five.

- Go to the *find friends* option (usually it's on the right of the home screen, under your profile) and use one of the contact imports to invite people to be your friend on Goodreads. The effectiveness of this will, of course, depend upon the number of people who follow / have friended you on twitter, facebook etc.

- Now click groups and go find a reader group or two that deals with your writing genre. For example, you might browse through the categories and drill down to The Mystery, Crime, and Thriller Group. It's an open group so one click to join and you're in. Take a look through the group guidelines and then browse the various chat threads under the different categories. Observe how people interact, their use of links to titles and author names, and the demarcation between reader and author activity. The guidelines under the Author's Corner put it succinctly: *When you are posting in this folder you are wearing your author's hat. When you post in any other folder please don your reader's hat and become one of us.*

- When you find a group that you are comfortable with, join the group and make your introduction according to the group guidelines. Be friendly, confident and engaging. Tell the group a little about yourself as reader and author.

- Once you have your own novel published, don't hesitate to add it to your own bookshelf. When you've done that you can become a Goodreads author. The Goodreads help section contains details under Author Program. It's free of charge and, once you've completed your author page with bio, blog links etc, it becomes another level in your social networking platform.

Goodreads is a rich resource and great fun. What does need taking into consideration is the high volumes of activity. You could easily spend your life on Goodreads, so your efforts need to be targeted. Manage your email notifications efficiently and be sure to respond promptly to any communications, either direct messages or on group threads that you participate in.

LibraryThing

LibraryThing is another huge online reading website. It's very similar in a lot of ways to Goodreads with bookshelves, reviews, groups, user and author profiles. One limitation of LibraryThing is you can't have more than 200 books on your shelf without a paid membership (at $25 for life, it's not expensive). One advantage of LibraryThing is that they allow Member Giveaway of ebooks, whereas Goodreads only allow paper books to be given away. In either case, it's a good way of stimulating interest in your book and, although member reviews are not mandatory for giveaways, they usually produce a good yield of reviews that will then be posted on the originating site and anywhere else that the member is active.

Gravatar

Gravatar stands for Globally Recognised Avatar. When you want to make a comment on a blog or website you will find that Gravatar.com is a very useful tool for keeping your brand on display. Upload your bio, avatar and contact details to Gravatar and confirm your identity by linking to different components of your social network. This will enable your details to come up whenever you make a comment on a blog or website.

Other social networks

Facebook and twitter are just two social networks. There are a number of others such as Google+ and LinkedIn. Many authors are beginning to get to grips with Google+ and I sometimes see LinkedIn mentioned. A couple of years ago all the big noise was MySpace. The point I'm making is you need to keep on your toes regarding which social networks you use. Google+, LinkedIn and others might work well for you. If you hear through the grapevine that a different social network is working for an author friend then go and take a look. The principles are the same – each part of your platform must complement the other so the whole is more than the sum of the parts.

A word of warning about your social networking platform! Social networking is a high intensity, high energy activity. It can be all too easy to leap from email inbox to facebook, check your blog, write a blog post, tweet it, check your Goodreads and go back around the never-ending circle. Before you know it, your social networking can impinge upon your creative writing time. Allocate a certain maximum amount of daily time to your network activities and stick to the limit. Otherwise you may fall victim to Compulsive Communication Syndrome. Read Vignette 2 below and learn from my mistakes.

~~~

Vignette 2 - Compulsive Communication Syndrome

This item was originally posted May 22nd 2011 on the Ruby Barnes blog and is a major lure for elephant hunters.

A guy sits in a field in Kansas, repeatedly clicking his fingers. Click, click, click.

A woman walks up to him and asks why he's compulsively clicking his fingers.

'To keep the elephants away,' he says.

'But there are no elephants in Kansas,' the woman says.

'See!' the guy says, 'It works.'

When I first read that joke in *Abnormal Psychology* by David S Holmes I thought myself immune to such behaviour. I had no aversion to elephants and couldn't even click my fingers. I had tried to learn how to click my fingers. God, how I'd tried. Again and again and again.

It was the last decade of the millennium; internet and email had yet to become commonplace in 1991. But something was in the ether that would eventually put me into my own elephant zone.

Compulsive Communication Syndrome - the symptoms

Fast forward to 2011, and here I sit with two computers switched on and fully loaded. Windows phone. A cup of tea. A glass of water. Two dirty coffee cups and a sandwich plate full of crumbs. A black & white LaserJet printer. A colour LaserJet printer. Wait, where's my scanner? At the office where I left my other computer with the docking station and widescreen LCD. What am I wearing? Let's just say last century down & out and mountain man hair.

There's a ringing noise. Sounds like, no, it can't be. Do we still have a landline? How quaint. Too late. I can see from the display that it was my wife. She'll be on her way home for a lunch I haven't yet prepared. In my defence, I'm off sick with viral influenza so she can't expect too much.

Just check my TweetDeck again, programme a few more chuckles and product plugs. Fly over to facebook, nice to see that some people have 'liked' my comments about Stephen Leather's post of the man from Washington State who claims to have had sex with over 1000 cars. Offer virtual friendship (to the 'likers' not the 1000 autolover man). Two new friend requests, trawl through their photos. Accept.

Windows phone is flashing, email via work and hotmail. Touch mousepads to activate the laptops, enter passwords. Oh. Real world calling. Car is due a service and teeth are due a dental check-up. Both very overdue. Where do these people expect me to find the time? Pick up landline, because I want to see the mobile flash if I get any ReTweets or Direct Messages. Book the car in with the hygienist and the teeth for a 15,000 mile lube.

Madame's still not home so I have a chance to read two pages of Virtual Strangers on Kindle for PC, then over to the other laptop. Edit the section of The Baptist to make the intimate tattoo more believable, having sought semi-professional advice at 2:30 this morning from a lovely facebook lady who chats about these things.

Tweet *I just completed the intimate tattoo scene #iamwriting*.

And...cut. That's a wrap. A coleslaw, beetroot and mushroom wrap with mayonnaise. Cup of tea. Quick snooze. Lovely wife's gone back to work, I can stop acting sick and get back into the swim.

I prepare myself for the weekly kindle book tagging exercise and copy paste the list of 200+ books and tags into a Word doc so I can do it while we're watching CSI tonight. Then I remember that I've withdrawn from the tagging group. I feel hollow, the tagging was fun. In the way that in my temp job, way back when, converting London numbers from 01 to 071 and 081 was fun. Supermarket checkout, repetitive, result producing fun. The copy, open link, paste, save times 200+ and the excitement of seeing Peril as number 5 tagged crime novel on amazon.com.

Unfortunately it doesn't translate into sales so that's why I've stopped the tagging.

And there it is. A piece of evidence. I have made a positive decision to not engage in a social networking activity because I don't see the specific benefit I was looking for.

Just before any social networking authors jump down my throat and say stuff like *it all has to be part of a cohesive marketing palette* or something similarly artistic, the point I want to make is not about tagging. It's that I managed to stop doing something. I can't stop the other stuff. What can stop the other stuff is a flat battery, breakdown of the broadband, breakdown of facebook / twitter / Blogger, one of my children needing medical care, power cuts or an offer of sex. All of which are increasingly rare events.

The rationale

So why, oh why, am I compulsively 'building a social network platform' every spare second of the day and night? Because I am an independent author with my crime novel Peril on Kindle and Smashwords. And with a very tasty further work in the pieline. (It's the pies and the typos that are slowing it down.) Or is this just my latest justification for compulsive behaviour? Now that I've built the platform to Kristen Lamb's *WANA* prescription for critical mass, can I tame my behaviour? The facebook friends, twitter followers and blog readers are mushrooming nicely. So I should be able to just tickle occasionally, right?

Wrong, with a big wobbly W. Wronger than a toilet roll hung the wrong way.

When Dad brought home a Binatone TV tennis game (in the 1970's, humour me) I had to be dragged off it after a week. The first time on a Space Invaders machine in the pub I drank no beer and chatted no girls the whole evening. I recognised the problem at that stage. A compulsive personality trait that could put me on a treadmill without end. Like collecting pictures of Page 3 girls, er, I mean stamps. So I studiously avoided anything that looked like a compulsive lure. Stayed away from Space

Invaders and all similar things ever since, never played fruit machines, X-Box, PC games or anything that seemed to drag others in. I've rarely bet on the horses or gambled in casinos. Just once, okay twice, at Dublin's Sporting Emporium where a Brazilian transsexual's roulette method netted me €450 (thanks Joel, big kiss X, and if you want to know the simple, foolproof method then read Peril).

Addiction

A lot of people ruin their lives with compulsive behaviour. If it's substance consumption, then that's clinically an addiction. Dr Larch in *The Cider House Rules* by John Irving was addicted to ether but most people think of addiction as drink or drugs. Clinicians wouldn't agree that gambling, game playing or internet social networking is an addiction, but that's just nomenclature. If not physically addictive, it is psychologically addictive for individuals with compulsive tendencies. That includes me and, as you're reading this, possibly you and all those hundreds, thousands and gazillions of users on facebook, twitter, Blogger, Wordpress and other web places.

Robert palmer used to sing *Might as well face it, I'm addicted to love*. Actually Rob, if your claims were true, you technically had a borderline compulsive personality disorder that led to excessive passion (RIP coolest dude ever). But let's call it addiction because, like Rob, we can't stop doing it. We feel bad if we don't do it. It's part of what we are. It's what we do.

Secrecy and paranoia

The urge to communicate is very strong. I was waiting in a doctor's surgery the other day and a chap in a suit pulled out an iPhone. He spent his twenty minutes, before the nurse did whatever she was going to do to him, surfing on facebook. From the few pictures I saw I doubt very much that his wife (he wore a ring) would have approved. I must get one of those phones. And that leads into another destructive aspect of compulsive communication syndrome. Secrecy. Guarding of passwords, logins, enabling and disabling cookies, deleting history. Alt Tab to switch screens at a touch if an unauthorised person (man, woman or child) comes too close to your screen.

Compulsive communication on social media is often outside of the direct family and friends circle. It has an element of fantasy or 'other life' to it. There's a danger of driving a wedge between you and the actual real humans that surround you. And if you are unable to fully conceal your activities, and you won't, then there's a risk of engendering paranoia in those you love, including yourself.

One writer friend said to me the other day 'My husband is always on his Blackberry. Drives me crazy with it, he does.'

A couple of days later, I was in a local hotel having lunch with my extended family. Out of nowhere my wife shouted at me across the crowded room. 'Who the hell are you texting or emailing or whatever it is that you do with that thing?'

I had both hands under the table and shamefully produced an oblong coffee biscuit in a black plastic wrapper that I was struggling to open. The look on her face said *you've got away with it this time, but I know what you're up to. Okay, I don't know what you're up to but I'm sure you're up to no good.*

If you have ever written or read the words *have to go, my partner just walked in* then you run the risk of valuing virtual relationships over real ones. Exciting though, isn't it?

Communities, threads, peer pressure, trolls and flame wars

There's more. All of these social networking platforms abound with virtual cafés and nightclubs where readers, writers and, well, anybody really, can participate. There are valuable aspects of writers' craft, and marketeers' witchcraft discussed. People exchange witticisms and genuine, if virtual, friendships are made (and sometimes lost). Folks even fall into and out of virtual love. But, like drivers of cars, web users are insulated from each other by the ether and if someone is touchy, aggressive, having a bad day, drunk or a semi-professional bad-ass, then flame wars can erupt on threads and forums.

21st century trolls stalk cyberspace, sniffing out the weak and wounded. Like Shrek they delight in provoking the villagers into a troll hunt and enjoy consuming everyone in the posse, bones and all. When you find yourself having an 'offline' email exchange with a forum member about whether or not to feed a troll then you are likely very, very far away from producing actual creative writing as an author. And the likelihood that you can credibly explain to your partner or family the virtuous goal you are pursuing with all this time consuming activity is small, titchy, infinitesimal.

I'm currently reading *Virtual Strangers* by Susanne O'Leary and Ola Zaltin. It's a very interesting crime novel that gives an insight into the *Authorspot* (Authonomy) website for budding new writers. Autho is a huge site with thousands of active users engaging in a whirl of social networking. The objective is to get into the top five of several thousand new novels that are uploaded to the site at any time. The top five novels of the month receive a professional critique from Harper Collins Publishers, who run the site.

Virtual Strangers is fiction but it gives a glimpse of the compulsive behaviour involved in climbing to the pinnacle of a peer review site. Some sites are less of a beauty contest and more of a structured peer review arrangement, but the compulsion kicks in just the same. Learning by reviewing is a great tool for a budding author. It's also a great rationale for compulsive participation.

And what are authors doing when they're reading and reviewing or 'backing' other people's work? They're not writing. If you're an author and you get to the point where you think *hey, I'm a really good reviewer, perhaps I could be an editor*, then quite possibly you are but you're eating into your own valuable writing time.

Is there a cure?

If compulsive social networking is ruining your life, then what's the answer? Is there really a *Mark Zuckerberg Clinic* as in *Virtual Strangers*? Some people I know have left their compulsion behind. Usually by accepting that their perceived goal has been achieved, that it was just an excuse or by realising that the goal is ultimately unachievable within reasonable expectations (that sounds like nonsense but then...)

So, how did they leave it behind? Cold turkey is the answer.

Others have been forced by extreme personal circumstances to get a grip and adjust their priorities. Most people I've met in this otherworld are still here, buzzing.

Sorry, I just don't agree with any of this...

What's supposed to be the problem here? Everybody texts using mobile phones, listens to their mp3 player when in a crowd, works the virtual room on facebook and stuff like that. We nearly all use computers in the workplace and there's as much or more communication by email than phone. Right?

Right. Except that employers have imposed strong restrictions on employee internet access because they know that their humans will spend all day on facebook, twitter and other stuff if the temptation is left open.

I managed to studiously avoid social network platforms, up until late 2009, because I heard the Space Invader warning sound in my head. If I entered the wonderful, magic forest I might never come out again. In November 2009 a writer friend lured me onto Authonomy to back her book and, within about six weeks, I very nearly ruined the family Christmas with my compulsive participation. The dangers of addiction were so strong and clear that I did manage to pull free.

Then I moved to YouWriteOn and became addicted-lite to that, which was almost bearable for the family i.e. me moving out wasn't actually a discussion topic that time. But I got too deep into YWO as well. At the point where I thought I was an editor and no longer an author, I had a very stiff talking-to from my mentor and she bounced me over the YWO wall, to run free of obligations to other writers.

Having made two incursions and escapes, I decided to participate in the ebook revolution and, like many, conducted some research. I chose to follow Kristen's WANA suggestions and built up my social platforms. That was a very intense and compulsive exercise and it has me hooked.

If I'm serious about marketing my indie crime novels Peril and The Baptist then I know there are some further things I have to do, such as blog-hopping and blog tours. A friend has given me some suggestions on how to approach that with the caveat 'Good luck, and get ready to have your life consumed'. That has Space Invaders written all over it.

Have to go, *my partner just walked in.*

~~~

RUBY BARNES

Part 3 - Publishing an independent ebook

At last you've reached the point of publishing! It's a scary moment. You're going to bare your writer's soul to the public. You will be judged as an author, silently or vocally, by those who read it. Have no fear, because your novel has been work-shopped, edited, beta-read, proof-read and French polished. If it hasn't then you're not ready to self-publish. The first impression's the last impression; I know.

This section of the book describes independent ebook publishing. It doesn't handle independent paper publishing. That's for another day. At time of writing, some independent authors are achieving substantial and consistent success with their ebooks, depending upon the quality of their work and the degree of market exposure. The same doesn't necessarily hold true for independent paper publishing, which is usually done through the Print on Demand (POD) route. It's ebooks that have opened the market for us independent authors.

There's more than one way to convert your masterpiece into an ebook. Some how-to guides advise the use of conversion programmes to transform your electronic manuscript into an ebook file format. Others offer clever html templates into which you paste your manuscript text or they may even take you deep into re-writing the whole document as an html file. If that's what you want to do then thank you for your time and I hope you enjoyed parts 1 and 2 of this guide. On the other hand, if you want an easy way to take that manuscript and see it published as an ebook without having to dabble in complexity, then read on. We're going to keep it simple. Why? Because ereaders work best with simple, cleanly formatted ebooks. Even mainstream publishers screw up with conversion of their books to ebook format. Keep it simple.

You will need to have the following components to hand and remember, **version control is essential for all your docs**.

Your manuscript

You need the final version, as polished as you and your editing buddies can make it, as an electronic document, ideally in MS Word. Unless you are an author with incredible self-control, it's likely that your document will have a plethora of text styles, sizes and fonts. You might be one of the naughty people who use tabs or spaces to indent your paragraph first lines. MS Word is probably placing squiggly red and green lines all over your pages, telling you that your spelling and grammar is incorrect although it looks fine to your eyes. Don't worry about that, we're going to deal with it.

Your title

Fresh and memorable, it encapsulates your novel. Finding a unique and relevant title is almost impossible and there is no copyright on titles. If you choose a title that is already popular under another established author then you might ride on the popularity of that existing title or you might sink into the low ranks of search engines. Search the internet and Amazon using your intended title and see what comes up. You might want to try out alternative titles on selected reader / writer friends. Once you've decided then stick with that title.

A professional-looking front cover

You need this as a jpg file. The cover should be a visual synopsis of your novel, immediately communicating the one big idea of the book. It needs to work at both full cover size on an ereader and at thumbprint size for web presentation. My suggestion is to browse your genre on Amazon and pick five or ten covers that you think are really good. Save them to your computer (right click, save image) and flick through them. If you are thinking of designing your own cover then would you be able to emulate those covers? If not then don't try.

An amateurish cover will likely deter potential readers from even sampling your writing. There are any number of good cover designers willing to create something individual for prices from $30 up. Ask friends on your social network for recommendations but, before you go with a designer, first check out their previous work. Then, before settling on final cover design, ask friends and peers for their honest opinion. It can be very difficult to extract that honest opinion but, if and when you update, folk won't hesitate to tell you the old one stank but they didn't like to say so at the time.

A product description

Also known as a blurb, your description intrigues, entices and hooks potential readers. If you pick up a print book and read the back cover then it should immediately impress upon you what genre the novel is in, the main themes of the story and what sort of a ride the reader is in for. Your product description is a written version of the visual impression given by your front cover. It doesn't have to be a synopsis, in fact you mustn't include any spoilers, but it does need to tantalise. There will be opportunities to fine tune this description.

Amazon and Smashwords allow up to 4000 characters in the book description, which is somewhere around 750 words, but you need to hit hard and fast in the first few lines to grab the reader's attention. Smashwords also has a 400 character short description which is the blurb that will appear on the front page of channels that Smashwords distributes to.

Tags / keywords

These will identify your novel in a search. Have at least seven of these to hand. These keywords should answer the question 'what sort of book is this?' Examples of tags for *The New Author* are *authorship, creative writing, e-publishing, epublishing, facebook, formatting guide, indie publishing, novel writing, publish my novel, self-publishing, social media, twitter, writing 101, writing skills, digital publishing.*

Setting expectations

Now you have all the material you need to epublish your book. The process will take anything from a couple of days to a couple of weeks, depending upon how many snags you hit. So be patient, be determined, pay attention to detail and **ensure to observe version control and backup for all your docs at all times** (I can't emphasise this point enough).

There are numerous retail outlets for ebooks and as many ways in to the virtual bookshelves but we're going to go in via two straightforward routes: Amazon KDP and Smashwords. Follow the simple steps below and you will soon have your ebook for sale on Amazon, Barnes and Noble, iTunes, Sony, Kobo, Diesel and other ebook websites.

Getting your manuscript into shape for publishing

This is the key step for publishing your ebook. Everything else that follows is just websites, menus and options. The cornerstone of your endeavour is a cleanly edited and formatted ebook document.

Your manuscript is in its 'final' version. This means that your beta readers have done their job, all line edits are complete, you have run spell and grammar checks, and read the entire finished thing through. MS Word has told you that some of your sentences are grammatically incorrect, but you have chosen to ignore that advice when it would wreck your author style and voice. What the checks won't tell you is when you have the spelling and grammar correct butt their [double sic] is a homonym. Watch out for this most common of indie author errors. Also watch out for different language settings creeping into your manuscript. If pedalling your bicycle suddenly gets corrected to pedaling, and agonizing to agonising, then you have some sections of text with language set to English (U.S.) and others to English (U.K.) or similar.

You are, at this point, probably heartily sick of your novel and desperate to get it off your computer and into the world. So let's do that together.

Open your Word doc

I'm going to make the big assumption that your manuscript is in MS Word. For those that are throwing apples at me, it's not the end of the world. Human propensity for mixing up formats in a document of some 70,000+ words is probably anyhow going to necessitate us applying the nuclear option and whacking our entire manuscript through a text editor. Let's take a look first at what we've got.

Make sure that your toolbar in Word includes the formatting buttons Style, Font and Font size, and the standard button ¶ Show/Hide (that backwards P known as the Pilcrow).

Scroll through some random pages throughout your manuscript and note how many different styles pop up in the Style box. Note any variation in Font Size. You will likely have a wide variety of styles and sizes. Now click on the Pilcrow and what do you see?

Are there dots being used for indentation of text? That's you using the space bar instead of first line indent.

Are there arrows? That's you using Tab instead of indent or alignment.

Are there Pilcrows in between paragraphs and lines, or a bunch of them at the top or bottom of pages? That's you using carriage return instead of line and paragraph spacing.

All of these things need to be eradicated and your manuscript simplified, because they can all lead to unpredictable results when translated into an ebook. Text alignment could end up all over the place, blank pages will appear in the ebook, some chapter headings won't be in your table of contents.

Now, it may be that your formatting is already perfect and none of the above issues present themselves. In that case, you're a better wo/man than I am and I undertake to tattoo your first name on my body where it's normally covered by clothes. You can choose the body part. But I'm prepared to bet my pristine epidermis that you have uncovered more than a smidgen of formatting issues.

Now you are presented with two choices; either address every formatting issue that you find (there are ways to do this with Alt / Edit / Find / Replace, selecting all instances of each style and updating) or else go for what is known as the nuclear option. To preserve your sanity and save time, I recommend the latter.

The Nuclear option

This approach will completely cleanse your manuscript.

- Simply go to Edit / Select All (or Ctrl A) and then Ctrl C to copy the entire text of your manuscript to the clipboard.

- Now open a text editor such as Notepad and Ctrl V to paste the entire text of your manuscript from the clipboard into that text editor. Then Ctrl A to select all of that text from the editor.

- Close down Word. Now open Word again and a new blank document will appear. Don't paste in your text yet. First make sure that the AutoCorrect and Autoformat options are unchecked in Tools > AutoCorrect Options > Autoformat > Apply (uncheck the four boxes) and in Tools > AutoCorrect Options > Autoformat As You Type (uncheck all boxes). If you don't do this then Word is going to tie you in knots and re-complicate your nuked manuscript.

- Now Hit Ctrl V and your entire manuscript is pasted into that new document, with all formatting removed, in the text style Normal. Save it with a name that tells you what you have done e.g. 'Nuclear The New Author v1.doc'.

The good news is that every formatting problem you had has been eradicated. The not so good news is that all formats for chapter titles, subtitles, bold and italics have also been eradicated. This is less of a problem for a novel than for a non-fiction work which is likely to be full of headings and sub-headings (like the book you're reading right now!) Any bullets and numbers will have been converted to text components rather than format.

Your next step is to go through this nuclear version of your novel and, very carefully and methodically, adjust it to exactly how you want your finished ebook to look like.

Reformat your nuked manuscript

Or re-clothe your naked manuscript. Bring up the Styles and Formatting menu and adjust the Normal style to whatever you want your body text to be. My suggestion is as follows.

Font: Times New Roman, Size 12, Left Aligned, Indent First Line: 0.5cm (or 0.25 inches), Line Spacing: 1.5, Space After: 6pt, Automatically Update

That will give your novel text a natural book-type presentation when viewed on an ereader. Fiction usually uses first line indent. If you prefer a different font, indent or spacing then you can adjust to your preferences but don't deviate too far, don't use fancy fonts and don't use page breaks for your normal text. Don't use block alignment, that's just for print books. Keep it simple.

Be aware that what you create in this Word manuscript will be displayed differently in different ereaders. That's why it's best practice to keep things simple.

If you feel the need to use block paragraph instead of first line indent, then you need to be aware that Amazon Kindle devices and apps automatically display with a first line indent. The way around this is to use a first line indent of 0.01 which will give the block effect on the reader. (This and numerous other detailed tips are contained in the *Smashwords Style Guide* which is a great resource for ebook formatting and a must-read for those planning to go the Smashwords route.)

Now format your chapter headings and sub-headings by allocating the Heading 1, 2 and 3 styles from the Styles and Formatting menu. You can modify these Heading styles if you wish, but again keep it simple. Don't make the text size too big and don't use fancy fonts. They are potential sources of error in the conversion to ebook.

Your manuscript is looking good. It's now tempting to get a bit clever and add a table of contents so that readers can jump to chapters by name. There are a couple of reasons why not to do this (although it is a good idea for non-fiction reference books like *The New Author*). Firstly, your reader doesn't know what your chapters contain and you want them to read your novel in sequence. Secondly, few if any print novels list the contents at the front. Check your bookshelves.

You want your ebook to emulate a print novel experience as closely as possible. If you really have to have that table of contents e.g. if mapping out the journey of your fantasy novel is helpful to the reader, then make sure that you don't include page numbers, because page numbers have no meaning in ebooks. The number of words on an ereader page depends upon the ereader user settings such as reading font size. In fact, ebooks are really a continuous document without fixed pagination except for page breaks.

Images in your manuscript

Maybe you also have the urge to include images in your ebook. Apart from the front cover, insertion of which depends upon whether using KDP or Smashwords, it's not a great idea to include images. More often than not, things will go wrong with conversion. Unless you have access to all the different ereaders in common use (kindle, Nook, Sony, iPhone etc), there is a risk that the ebook you produce might not display its content properly for the reader. Most print novels on your bookshelves don't contain images, so yours shouldn't either. Exceptions apply if maps or diagrams are essential to the reader experience.

Top and tail

Your novel is complete. It's time to sandwich it between the traditional opening and closing niceties.

You need a title page, copyright statement, a disclaimer and maybe a dedication. These will differ slightly between your Amazon kindle ebook and your Smashwords ebook, as Smashwords is prescriptive in its content requirements (more below in the Smashwords publishing section). If you look at the

Amazon top 100 kindle books, select a book and *Click to LOOK INSIDE*, you will see the sort of statements, disclaimers and dedications that authors favour. Decide what front matter you want for your ebook and make sure you handle the formatting with the same care as you have applied to the rest of your manuscript. Watch out in particular for text styles performing an auto-update when you create and format your front matter. You can easily undo the great work you have done so far.

Lastly, do you want to say farewell to your readers with THE END or will you take the opportunity to extend their intimate relationship with your writing? This is your chance to share About the Author, links to your social platform and, if you have one, a teaser for your next book. It's quite common these days for mainstream published authors to include personal contact information, even an email address (see the end of *The New Author* for examples).

Wrapping up

When you have completed everything above (**and remember version control!**), you have your Word document ready for conversion. Save it and now save it again as *file type Web Page, Filtered*. Word will give you a warning message that some MS Office features may be lost, but just click OK. You now have your finished and clean manuscript in the two formats that are needed.

Kindle Direct Publishing (KDP)

The majority of ebooks are sold by Amazon as azw files (compatible with the mobi file type) for reading on the Amazon kindle family of ereaders. There are also Kindle reader apps that can be used on laptops, smart phones and tablets. Amazon has opened the ebook door to independent authors by allowing them to upload, convert and market their writing via KDP. All genres and all forms are accommodated; short stories, novellas, novels, fiction and non-fiction. The only constraints are that the author has ownership of the work and the content doesn't breach decency guidelines (which are fairly flexible).

Go to *http://kdp.amazon.com* and register. If you have an existing Amazon account then you can use that login, otherwise set up as a new user. You will have to give personal details including home address, phone number and payment details (how they will pay you your commission on ebook sales. You don't have to pay them anything!). This is because you are entering into a contract with Amazon.

When your account details are completed you will be taken to your dashboard. Options at the top of the screen include Bookshelf, Reports, Community and KDP Select. Click on Bookshelf and then click Add new title. You have now entered the publishing process.

KDP Step 1 – Your book

KDP publishing is a 9 stage process that is displayed on two different screen pages. At time of writing, the first section of the page is about Kindle Select. You can read the information and decide at this stage whether to participate or else come back to it later. Kindle Select offers some marketing advantages in return for giving Amazon exclusive distribution rights to your ebook. If you do go ahead with Kindle Select then you won't be entitled to proceed with the Smashwords step below. Your choice.

1. Enter Your Book Details

Book name. It's crunch time. Your decision on the title of your novel must be made. The book name is what will appear on the Amazon page and also in Amazon searches. You can simply enter the title from your novel title page e.g. *Peril*, or you can add some extra e.g. *Peril: A Ger Mayes Thriller*. Don't succumb to the temptation to hype your book here with *Number One International Bestseller* or similar. Amazon may well refuse to publish. If your novel is part of a series then enter that information in the required fields.

Description. Paste in the blurb of up to 4000 words that you have pre-prepared for your novel. The text will be plain initially but, if required, you can format this at a later point through Amazon Author Central.

Add contributor. You need to add at least one contributor for your book and that is your name as author. Enter the name as you wish it to appear on your Amazon book page. If you wish to give credits to other contributors such as co-authors, editors or designers at this stage then do so, but be aware that they will get equal billing with you on your product page. An acknowledgment inside your book may be adequate.

Language defaults to English. **Publication date**, **Publisher** and **ISBN** fields are optional. If you have the urge to create a fictitious publisher then that might add credibility but be aware that people may then search for that publisher on the internet and the credibility will soon be undermined. An ISBN doesn't serve any useful purpose on Amazon. Your ebook will automatically be assigned an ASIN (Amazon Standard Identification Number) which is the key reference on Amazon.

2. Verify Your Publishing Rights

Click on *This is not a public domain work and I hold the necessary publishing rights*.

3. Target Your Book to Customers

Use the **Add categories** button to browse through the kindle store categories until you find where you want to place your ebook. You can select up to two categories.

Search keywords. Enter up to 7 words, separated by a comma, which you want to be the key words that will produce your ebook in an Amazon search. These keywords can be short phrases e.g. contemporary fiction, psychological thriller.

4. Upload your book cover

First decide if you want the image you upload to be included in the kindle file. If you tick this box then make sure not to also embed your front cover in your file, else there will be two front covers displayed on the purchaser's kindle. Now browse and upload your stunning front cover, minimum size 500 x 800 pixels, portrait orientation. This cover image will appear as the thumbnail in Amazon searches and as the cover visual on the ebook product page (plus also within your ebook if you check that option).

5. Upload your book file

Check *Enable digital rights management* if you don't want purchasers to share your book with other readers. Then browse to the HTML version of your manuscript. Kindle ebook files are html files, so loading as html ensures that your ebook will turn out the way you formatted it. Click on Upload book and the message *Converting book file to Kindle format* will appear. After a few seconds a green tick and the message *Upload and conversion successful* will appear. Your novel is now loaded into the KDP system.

6. Preview Your Book

There are two ways to preview your ebook on KDP. The first is the Simple Previewer. Click and you will see something that looks a bit like the *Click to LOOK INSIDE* function, except more basic. This emulates the Kindle screen, including variable font size. However, the way the text looks – indents, centred, breaks etc. – doesn't accurately reflect how it will look in the final ebook. It's only a quick check to ensure that things aren't too crazy.

Until recently Simple Previewer was the only previewer available, but KDP have recently added the Enhanced Previewer. Click on Download Book · Preview File and save the mobi file to your computer. You now need to look at that mobi file, ideally with an actual Kindle. If you don't possess a Kindle then download the Enhanced Previewer from KDP. The Enhanced Previewer has the advantage that it can emulate the presentation of your ebook on Kindle, Kindle Fire, Kindle DX, iPhone and iPad.

You know what's coming next. It can't be neglected. You need to page through your entire novel on your Kindle or Enhanced Previewer, checking the format. Look out for blank pages, incorrect line spacing, odd indents and any nonsensical characters. This is the final quality check of your ebook on KDP. The entire onus for quality control on KDP rests with the author. The system will let you publish rubbish. After this the next person to read your novel will be a paying customer and they will judge your professionalism based upon product content and presentation, so make sure it is as good as you can get it. There's no point in eating the cow and choking on the tail.

Save and Continue. This will take you to the second step of the KDP process.

KDP Step 2 - Rights & Pricing

7. Verify Your Publishing Territories

As your novel is your own work you will have global distribution rights. This section allows you to choose the countries in which you authorise Amazon to sell the Kindle version of your book. If you have no particular reasons not to sell in some territories, then click Worldwide rights – all territories. Otherwise select just those countries you wish to sell in. At time of writing, Amazon has dedicated Kindle web stores on amazon.com, amazon.co.uk, amazon.de, amazon.fr, amazon.es and amazon.it. By default, all countries outside of US, UK, Germany, France, Spain and Italy (with some exceptions of countries closely associated e.g. by language) must buy their kindle books from amazon.com.

8. Choose Your Royalty

There are two royalty options, depending upon price thresholds, and you can tie the selling price to US$ or set separately in £ and €.

35% royalty is available on ebooks priced from US$ 0.99 to US$ 200.00 / £0.75 to £120.00 / €0.86 to €173.91. In fact, most indie ebooks are priced somewhere between 99c and $5.99.

70% royalty is available on ebooks priced within an interim price band of between $2.99 and $9.99 / £1.49 and £6.99 / €2.60 and €8.69. (Yes, there's an overlap between the 35% and 70% price bands so choose with care.)

The royalty option you select will be applied to all Amazon sites. It's not possible to use the 35% model for low pricing in one country and the 70% model for higher pricing in another territory on the same ebook. It can be varied for other ebooks when you have them ready.

You can change your choice of royalty option and pricing at any time after publication, with a delay of a few hours before it changes on Amazon. There is substantial online debate about pricing of ebooks and the decision lies with you as author. 99c will net you 35c or thereabouts per ebook sale. $2.99 will net you $2.07 or thereabouts (Amazon may deduct a small amount for transmission costs). Volume of sales is likely to be higher at lower price. You may want to establish a broader readership with the 99c minimum price or even free initiatives such as KDP Select, or you might ally the 70% commission with a view that your work is worth more than a coffee. I'll leave it there.

9. Kindle Book Lending

This is optional if you have selected the 35% royalty. If you've gone for the 70% royalty then your book is enrolled, no choice. The lending feature allows purchasers of your ebook to lend to other people for up to 14 days, during which they themselves can't read the ebook.

Save and Publish

The next step is going to put your ebook up on the Amazon web store. There's a tick box and then you have to click the *Save and Publish* button. It's worth checking over Your Book and Rights & Pricing one last time before you publish, as your ebook will be inaccessible for 24 to 72 hours during the initial publishing. Click *Save for later* and check through the above steps again. Then finally *Save and Publish*.

That's it! Your ebook is going to appear on Amazon in the next couple of days. Go back to your Bookshelf and you will see your ebook title with an ASIN (Amazon Standard Identification Number) underneath in brackets. That ASIN is unique and the key reference for your book. Your title is unavailable for any further modification until the In Review status turns to Live. If you do subsequently make changes then they will take effect within around 12 hours.

Amazon will email you once your title is published on the web but if you want to be obsessive about checking for it in the interim then use the ASIN.

It's a good idea to go and purchase your own ebook to check the end result but you will only be able to do this once with your customer ID. What gets delivered to your Kindle or Kindle for PC will be an azw file (this is the same as the mobi format that you previewed).

Further Amazon KDP features

Before we move on to publishing with Smashwords, there are three other Amazon subjects to be covered.

KDP Reports

The Reports section of KDP gives you sight of your ebook sales numbers and royalties earned.

1. Month-to-date Unit Sales

This is where all the newbies spend far too much time! Your cumulative unit sales will appear onscreen against the title and ASIN. Sales numbers aren't time-stamped. This tends to make some KDP authors feel like they have to check this report on an hourly basis or even more often. But remember, a watched pot never boils.

There's a column on the report that shows Units Refunded. It's unlikely that you will get many counts in this column. It signifies customers that have electronically returned their purchase. The cause of returns is usually a mistaken purchase i.e. they probably accidentally hit the *Buy now with 1-Click* button. If you have your ebook set to free via KDP Select, or forced free by Amazon price comparison bots, returns sometimes occur from people who are scooping up freebies and find yours not to their taste. During my KDP free periods I've experienced a return rate of around 1 in 2000 copies.

If you participate in KDP Select then you can see the resulting Units Borrowed and Free-Units Promo.

Units Borrowed earns a lending fee for the author but Free-Units Promo earns no royalties.

Free Units-Price Match shows the number of royalty-free ebook copies that were sold for zero price during a price match by the Amazon pricing bots.

The Month-to-date unit sales report isn't real time. There's a variable time lag of around half an hour up to several hours depending upon who knows what. And sometimes the report can systemically malfunction for half a day or so. Another reason not to sit staring at the screen!

2. Prior Six Weeks' Royalties

This report shows ebook sales and royalties earned per week during the previous six weeks. The week ending date is the Saturday and figures are reported a week in arrears. Each country site is reported separately.

Depending upon your sales price, royalty level and domicile, it may take a few months before Amazon is in a position to send your first royalty cheques / transfers. For example: UK authors with ebooks on Amazon.com need to reach a cumulative royalty of $100 + withholding tax before they will receive a postal cheque; US authors can receive royalties by bank transfer for payments above $10 from Amazon.com; UK / Ireland authors can receive royalties for amounts above £10 by bank transfer from Amazon.co.uk.

3. Prior Months' Royalties

This provides Excel downloads per month of all sales for the previous twelve months. Each separate Excel file covers one month and lists all sales for that month per ebook title per country site. Reports are generated by the 15th day of the following month.

KDP Community

Click on Community in your dashboard and you will be taken to the KDP Community forums. KDP authors pose and answer questions on all kinds of topics, mostly KDP related. Browse a few of the forums to see how the discussions run and what sort of content is included. If you wish to participate in any forum threads, or start your own, you will need to log in and create a nickname. Choose carefully as this nickname cannot be changed later. My choice was Ger Mayes, the main character of my first novel, and I missed a branding opportunity when I didn't choose Ruby Barnes as my nickname. I suggest that you use your author name so that folks can easily find you on social networks and search for your books on Amazon without a link.

The usual chat forum guidelines apply. Get a feel for the protocol. Introductions aren't usually necessary but members don't appreciate hit and run advertising by authors, unless the thread specifically invites authors to do so. Be courteous but confident and pay back any favours. Remember you're a newbie and respect the input of more experienced members. Don't rise to the bait of any aggressive or inappropriate behaviour. The community is monitored by Amazon KDP and they will step in if required.

The KDP Community is quite different to most other communities. Most everyone is a self-published author. A few are in process but haven't yet hit the Save and Publish button. Bear in mind that there are very few quality controls on KDP publishing and the standard of ebooks is very variable. You will meet critically acclaimed independent authors that have sold tens or hundreds of thousands of ebooks and have a stable of titles. At the other end of the spectrum you'll bump into new authors with work of questionable quality and an attitude problem. Those individuals are usually identifiable by their tendency to rant.

So why bother with this KDP Community thing? The reason is to tap into the huge depth of knowledge amongst the KDP authors and they like to share. Almost any question you might ask has already been covered and members will happily guide you to it or answer afresh.

The two most used forums are **General Questions** and **Voice of the Author / Publisher**. One of the best threads for marketing advice is titled *What Mioves Kindle books off the shelf?* and its sister thread with the suffix 2 (spelling mistake of *Mioves* is the actual thread name and you can learn from this – the name of a thread, once started, can't be edited). Every KDP author who has an opinion to share on how to market ebooks has contributed to the thread and it's worth taking some hours over the course of a few days to read through and make some notes.

If you do contribute to any thread then don't miss the opportunity to add an Amazon link to your book or your blog address or twitter name. If what you say is of interest to others then they may well join your social network and / or take a look at your ebook. I've made some good virtual friends through KDP Community.

Remember that KDP Community is an author community. Some of the members will look at your book and some might even buy it, but they are not your target market. You can ask people to look at your ebook page on Amazon and give you feedback on the cover, product description or sample (from *Click to LOOK INSIDE*), but don't throw out ads for your book like junk mail. It will simply be ignored or worse.

Some members engage in mutual reviews of ebooks. I would recommend against such a mutual appreciation society. At best you will get a positive review from a fellow indie author. At worst you will get a sycophantic five star review that doesn't look genuine and their book will not be to your liking, leaving you in a difficult position regarding your credibility as a reviewer and author. There's also a risk that you'll end up spending a lot of time reading and reviewing other authors' work, which isn't what you should be doing. During all of the above process, you should spend at least some time busy writing your next manuscript.

There are numerous opportunities on KDP Community to broaden your social network, do blog interviews and post your book on various indie author websites. As long as you don't spend too much of your valuable time engaged in such activity, it's worth doing.

Amazon Author Central

Once your ebook is published on Amazon there are some finishing touches to be made. Go to *authorcentral.amazon.com* and join up. You can use your regular Amazon login and password.

The first step is to enter your author name. The system will identify your book and ask if you are the author. Once you confirm a confirmation email will then be sent to you. Click on that and you will come to your books page on Author Central.

Books

Click on your book cover and you will have a range of fields where you can add or adjust the product page of your ebook. Unlike during the KDP publishing process, you can now format your product description with bold, italics, numbers, bullets and even html. At time of writing this feature only works on authorcentral.amazon.com, not other author central country sites, but format changes are reflected onto the other sites. You can also add an About the Author text that will appear on your ebook product page.

Profile

Author Central allows you to build your Profile which will become your Author Page. That page is accessible to Amazon customers by clicking on your author name on your book page. Create your author page by adding a biography, pictures and social networking links (here's mine as an example: http://www.amazon.com/author/rubybarnes).

Sales Info

You can view a chart of your book's Amazon rating over time. This is of passing interest as it doesn't give you sales volume, which is available on KDP Reports.

Customer Reviews

All reviews posted on Amazon.com are listed on this page. As you add titles their reviews will also appear on the list. It's a useful place to read the reviews and copy snippets for use elsewhere but resist the temptation to add a comment to any review, especially negative reviews. Take any adverse reviews on the chin and accept that you can't please all the people all of the time. Any war of words with a reviewer always reflects badly on the author. If you receive a blatantly incorrect review then use *Contact Us* at the bottom of the Author Central page. Amazon respond very quickly and efficiently to Author Central queries.

Author Central in different countries

At the time I wrote this book, Amazon had different Author Central sites for each of the Kindle store countries: US, UK, DE, ES, FR, IT. Each of them requires a separate setup, claiming of books and author profile. The reviews are also held separately per country. (Note that formatting of product description should be performed via authorcentral.amazon.com.)

Amazon store

If you already buy books from Amazon then you will have an Amazon customer account. That account enables you to do a lot more than just purchase Amazon goods. Once logged in, you can like and tag books, leave reviews of books that you've read, and join discussions in reader and author forums. Each of these features is individual to the country site i.e. if you like a book, tag and review it, those actions only apply to that country site. Furthermore, you can only like, tag and review books on a country site from which you have purchased.

Like

There's a Like box just under the title on your Amazon ebook page. If nobody has liked your book then it does look a little unloved but there's no real evidence that a large number of likes will boost sales. Some indie authors participate in mutual like fests but it can look a bit fake if you have a ton of likes, very few reviews and a sales ranking of 500,000.

Tags

Way down the product page, past the More About the Author section (which will lead to the Profile that you posted via Author Central), are the tags. These are keywords that customers might search under. Again, there's no real evidence that a large number of tags will boost sales but a number of relevant and carefully chosen tags is essential for your ebook to appear in the relevant searches. Tagging is a very typical indie author back scratching exercise.

Amazon discussion forums

Down past the tags area you will find a selection of discussion forums that Amazon has chosen as relevant to your ebook's genre. There are a huge number of Amazon discussion forums, many of them Kindle related, and it can be a bit confusing trying to find a particular forum. Click on one of them and try using the forum search for keywords. Be aware, though, that Amazon has banned author promotion in almost all of these forums due to excessive ebook hit-and-run spam selling by over-anxious indie authors. Amazon moderates closely and will delete inappropriate posts and sometimes even ban authors from posting.

If you participate in an Amazon forum then the usual rules apply. Read some, discover the protocol, be courteous but confident and handle yourself with your reader hat on. Only put your author hat on in any forums that are specifically titled and introduced as an author forum.

That pretty much wraps up the Amazon epublishing experience. Amazon means Kindle and there are millions, perhaps tens of millions, of these devices now sold. The true figures are unknown. Any PC, Apple, smartphone or tablet user can use the Kindle apps. But there is also a huge market of millions that don't use the Kindle apps. Apple has its own iStore for ebooks and there are several other manufacturers of dedicated ereaders e.g. Barnes & Noble Nook, Kobo, Sony.

The task of placing your ebook directly with these other marketplaces ranges from achievable to impossible. For example, Barnes & Noble have their own publishing system called PubIt! but this is only accessible to US based authors and publishers. However, there is another way into these marketplaces; Smashwords.

Smashwords

An easy route into many ebook distribution channels, Smashwords enables authors to publish in a range of formats, to create discount vouchers and to gift ebooks. Smashwords is a product catalogue rather than a social network but it works well as a product hub and does gather product reviews.

Some authors don't participate in Smashwords because the site doesn't use Digital Rights Management (DRM). DRM-free means your book could theoretically be copied and distributed by readers without your permission and without compensation. The DRM-free approach is deliberate as Smashwords don't agree with the restrictive approach of DRM. Removing DRM allows a reader to place the ebook on multiple devices e.g. Kindle, PC, iPad / tablet / smartphone. They rely upon customers to honour the work of authors and purchase their own copy for their own use. This doesn't sit well with some authors who are worried about piracy. The fact of the matter is that even DRMed works can be easily pirated. My tuppence is that piracy will occur anyway and it is the province of the big boys (mainstream publishers, Amazon etc.) to set their legal eagles onto the pirates, which they successfully do. I choose to join the 100,000 plus ebooks on Smashwords and use their distribution channels. If I hadn't joined Smashwords then I would have around 2,000 fewer readers of my books in 2011.

The main strengths of Smashwords are threefold: your ebook can be distributed to various channels (providing you can format sufficiently well for their Premium Catalog) and you still earn a good level of royalty; Smashwords converts your Word doc into numerous ebook formats suitable for all kinds of ereaders; the coupon facility enables you to easily provide discounted or free copies of your ebook for review, competitions and promotions.

Register

Go to Smashwords.com and click on Join. Relatively few details are required at this stage and the confirmation email contains extensive introductory information that you should read carefully. There are numerous precious nuggets in there and links to key jump points on the Smashwords website. You can learn about formatting in the *Smashwords Style Guide*, read about how to market your ebook in *The Smashwords Book Marketing Guide* and browse all kinds of reader and author info on the site.

Mark Croker is the founder of Smashwords and author of those key articles and free guides I just mentioned. In his blog post *The Seven Secrets to Ebook Publishing Success* he more or less advocates the approach I've taken with *The New Author*: write a great book (or several); start building your marketing platform and social media strategy before you finish your book; epublish your book and leverage your platform to achieve viral promotion through word of mouth.

Now you've familiarised yourself with Smashwords, and possibly scared yourself if you've heard rumours of how difficult it is to get into the Premium Catalog,

I'm going to show you how to do it, nice and easy. You've done most of the hard work already.

Format your manuscript for Smashwords

Open the Word version of your wrapped up, ready for conversion manuscript. Now format your book title, copyright page and Smashwords license statement in line with the Smashwords guidelines. Here's an example (and there are further examples in the *Smashwords Style Guide*):

Book Title

FirstName LastName

Copyright 2010 by FirstName LastName

Smashwords Edition

Smashwords License Statement

This ebook is licensed for your personal enjoyment only. This ebook may not be re-sold or given away to other people. If you would like to share this book with another person, please purchase an additional copy for each reader. If you're reading this book and did not purchase it, or it was not purchased for your use only, then please return to Smashwords.com and purchase your own copy. Thank you for respecting the hard work of this author.

These components are essential if you wish your ebook to be approved for the Smashwords Premium Catalog, which is the route to distribution channels.

Publish your book

Click on Publish and a single page with 8 steps will open. Once you have completed this page and clicked the Publish button, your manuscript will go through the Smashwords Meatgrinder. This conversion programme will produce ebooks in all the formats that you have selected on this page. It will also give you feedback on whether there are outstanding issues with your submission. In order to get your ebook into Premium Catalog for distribution to channels (Barnes & Noble, Sony, Kobo, Diesel, Apple and others) you will need to rectify any outstanding issues. We'll come to that after these 8 steps. (There will be some repetition here, compared to the KDP section above, in case readers are only looking for Smashwords instructions.)

Step 1 - Title and synopsis

Title

It's crunch time. Your decision on the title of your novel must be made. The title is what will appear on the Smashwords page and also on the book page of distribution channels. You can simply enter the title from your novel title page e.g. *Peril*, or you can add some extra e.g. *Peril: A Ger Mayes Thriller*. Don't succumb to the temptation to hype your book here with *Number One International Bestseller* or similar. Some channels may refuse to publish.

Short description

You have up to 400 characters to give a short blurb. This is the short description that was mentioned at the start of Part 3 of this book. The guideline is one paragraph, complete sentences, no all-caps words and no links. About six lines of text maximum. This is your chance to hook readers as they browse. Smashwords will show this on your product page as Ebook short description. It also appears on Sony and Kobo.

Long description

This is the full length blurb of up to 4000 words that you have pre-prepared for your novel. The text will be plain without special formatting and will appear on Smashwords as Extended description. Everything that you would expect to find on the back cover or jacket of a print book should be in here. Again, no all-caps words, no links and no spoilers.

Language

Presumably you are writing in English. If not, then select your language so that purchasers will be advised. There are also different English versions available for selection: American, Australian, British etc.

Adult content

Smashwords allows readers and purchasers to place an adult filter on books. The adult content guideline is a bit subjective. Language, situations or images inappropriate for children under 18 years of age.

Step 2 - Pricing and sampling

There are three options here.

Make my book free

This will definitely gain you readership on different distribution channels but there are a couple of issues to consider if you want to go this route. The first is that Amazon have price-matching bots that crawl the internet and compare prices of products that are for sale on Amazon. If you choose free on Smashwords and the Amazon bot picks it up on a Smashwords distribution channel, for example Barnes & Noble, then Amazon might zap your KDP ebook sales price to zero. That in itself can be used as a strategy but a very uncontrollable one. The second issue is that different Smashwords channels take differing amounts of time to adjust to changes in Smashwords ebook details and pricing. Playing with Make my book free (or any price changes, in fact) runs the risk of having the same product priced differently in different web stores and without much control of timing.

Let my readers determine the price

This seems to be something of a legacy approach to ebook pricing. Barnes & Noble, one of the biggest ebooks sellers after Amazon, no longer accepts this pricing method so I would advise against it.

Charge a specific amount for my book

This is the same approach as KDP. Enter a sales price in here and you will see pie charts and figures showing the breakdown of costs and royalties for sales via Smashwords, affiliates (see Smashwords website for more details on affiliates) and Premium Catalog retailers. Compared with Amazon KDP, Smashwords offers a better royalty below the Amazon 70% threshold of $2.99. Above, Amazon give a better deal. If you want to compare then do so with the Amazon KDP royalty and the Premium Catalog royalty at a given price. Your Smashwords sales will be mostly through Premium Catalog retailers, direct Smashwords sales are rare.

However, it doesn't have to be either or with Amazon and Smashwords. Those Premium Catalog retailers are mostly serving a different cohort of readers, ones that don't use a Kindle or Kindle for PC etc. Barnes & Noble are likely to be your biggest Smashwords retailer and their customers read on the Nook device.

You can change your choice of royalty option and pricing at any time after publication, with an instantaneous change on Smashwords website and a delay of between a couple of days to a couple of weeks on Premium Catalog retailer sites. There is substantial online debate about pricing of ebooks and the decision lies with you as author. 99c will net you 59c per Premium Catalog ebook sale. $2.99 will net you $1.79. Volume of sales is likely to be higher at lower price. You may want to establish a broader readership with the 99c minimum price or even free pricing / vouchers, or you might take the view that your work is worth more than a coffee and price it at several dollars. I'll leave it there.

Sampling

You can enable sampling and set the percentage of free sample to be anywhere from 1 to 100%, offering a lot more flexibility than the free samples available on Amazon. Readers do pick up samples direct from Smashwords.

Step 3 - Categorization

Select a category for your book. The drop-down will automatically appear onscreen. You can select up to two categories but at least one is mandatory.

Step 4 - Tags

Enter key words that readers might search for. There is no limit to the number of tags but they will appear on your Smashwords ebook page, so best to keep them relevant and focused.

Step 5 - Ebook formats

The variety of formats on offer is a Smashwords strength. All the file types have their fans. Note that the mobi file type, as used by Kindle, is also listed. You can give vouchers for your ebook and be assured that readers will be able to find the format they desire on your Smashwords ebook page. If you want to restrict the formats provided for your ebook e.g. if you don't want RTF or Plain Text versions to be available, then untick the relevant box.

Step 6 - Cover Image

Smashwords automatically includes your cover image in your ebook file. So don't insert the cover image in your Word manuscript.

Now browse and upload your stunning front cover, minimum height 600 pixels, portrait orientation. This cover image will appear as the thumbnail on Smashwords searches and the ebook product page. Some of the Premium Catalog retailers e.g. Barnes & Noble, use quite large cover images on their ebook product page so your cover also needs to look good at larger than thumbnail size, even if you're not going to embed it in your ebook.

Step 7 - Select file of book to publish

Unlike Amazon KDP, Smashwords only accepts manuscripts in Microsoft Word. At this point you should have a cleanly formatted Word doc of your manuscript with cover picture (optional), title page, copyright statement, Smashwords License statement, your ebook novel content and whatever you have chosen to add at the back e.g. contact the author, teaser for next book. **Remember, version control and backup**. If you want to be totally thorough in maximising your chances of complete success with your first upload attempt then you should read and digest the *Smashwords Style Guide* and make sure that all recommendations are implemented. But, having followed the guidance in this book, you should already be pretty close. So go ahead and browse for your manuscript Word file.

Step 8 - Publishing agreement

There are some short statements that you implicitly accept by clicking the **Publish** button. You'll then receive the following onscreen message.

Your book has been received and is #xx in the queue

Depending upon the current level of publishing activity on Smashwords, the Meatgrinder processing of your ebook will take anything from two minutes to a few days (I've experienced both extremes). If your position in the queue is e.g. 100+ then best to just leave it run and go do something else. Continue writing your next book! Generally the process is much faster than Amazon KDP.

AutoVetter

Once the conversion is complete, you will receive an on-screen message and also an email. It's highly likely that you will receive something like the following:

Your book requires modification. AutoVetter detected one or more formatting errors you should correct now before we can add your book to the Premium Catalog for distribution to major retailers. The tips below will help you:

- *Copyright Page Error - Your book doesn't follow the copyright page recommendation in Step 21b of the Smashwords Style Guide Please see our FAQ, How to Fix the AutoVetter Copyright Error for quick examples.*

- *Hyperlinked Table of Contents Error - Please do not use Word's TOC field codes to construct your linked Table of Contents. Instead, per the step-by-step instructions in Step 20 of the Smashwords Style Guide, use Word's "Bookmark" feature.*

- *Cover image too small - We cannot distribute your book if the cover image doesn't meet retailer requirements. Cover images must be at least 600 pixels tall and wide. Cover images should be vertical rectangles, meaning that the height should be greater than the width.*

- *Paragraph separation error, mixing first line indent with before/after space in paragraph style.*

Your dashboard will show *Requires modification* in the Premium status column of your ebook. Clicking on that will take you to a list of any outstanding AutoVetter issues. You will need to fix any such issues to clear your ebook for review for Premium Catalog, which is where you want to be. Sometimes these issues are very small e.g. too many blank lines used for spacing, some text left in the header or footer section of one or more pages (remember, ebooks don't use headers or footers), generally aspects of formatting that have crept back into your document since you nuked it through a text editor.

If there are issues then the best action is to refer to the sections of the *Smashwords Style Guide* referenced by the AutoVetter, then try and identify them in your Word doc (turn on the Pilcrow ¶, it can help a lot to make problems visible). Alternatively you can go nuclear again. **Remember, version control and backup.**

At this point it's worth mentioning that most uploads don't pass the AutoVetter first time. Premium Catalog requirements are very stringent, much tougher than Amazon KDP which has really little or no quality control. Your ebook is, however, published on the Smashwords website at this point, warts and all. It's a good idea to *Click to unpublish* the ebook on your dashboard, just to keep it out of the Smashwords shop front until you are fully satisfied with the result.

Download the mobi and epub versions of your ebook

Go to your ebook product page and download the mobi and epub files. If you don't have a Nook, Apple device, Sony Reader or Kobo, then download Adobe Digital Editions for free and use that to view the epub file. Use your Kindle or Kindle for PC to view the mobi file. Step through each page of your ebook and try to spot the manifestation of those errors that AutoVetter has pointed out. Typically you will have random numbers or words appearing, indicating that you left headers and page number footers in the Word doc. Or you will have blank pages, indicating that you have used carriage returns instead of paragraph formatting to try and create white space. Things look quite different on an ereader compared with Word.

When those pesky AutoVetter errors have been ironed out, click *Upload new version* on your dashboard and browse to your refined Word doc. It may take another cycle or two before you find the blemishes that are causing AutoVetter to stumble. Once your ebook passes AutoVetter, it will automatically proceed to Premium Catalog.

Smashwords Premium status

The far right column on your dashboard shows your ebook's status with Premium Catalog. Click on this and you will find a red boxed message saying *Tasks awaiting your completion.*

This book is missing an ISBN. An ISBN is essential for distribution of your ebook to Apple, Sony and Kobo. Click on ISBN Manager and read the options.

I already have a new, unused ISBN. If you happen to have an ISBN that is not currently assigned to an existing ebook or print book then you can use that and the publisher will be shown on the ebook product page (Smashwords and Premium Catalog retailers) as whatever you enter in the Publisher Contact Information (fields appear on page if you click *I already have an new, unused ISBN*. This may not be an appealing option to you as a new, indie author unless you have aspirations of becoming a publisher.

Free ISBN! Smashwords will provide the ISBN and register themselves as the publisher and you as the author in the Bowker record, which is the USA ISBN registry. This is a free flag of convenience.

Premium ISBN — USD $9.95. Smashwords will handle the purchase and allocation of an ISBN for you that will show you as publisher and author in the Bowker record. Note that this option only applies to residents of the United States of America or US Territories. Smashwords gives this option but considers it a vanity ISBN.

Pending approval

Once your ebook makes it through the AutoVetter without any errors, the Premium status will change to Pending approval. It takes a week, give or take a couple of days, for the Smashwords team to review you ebook's suitability for distribution. This can be frustrating because you want the job finished so you can clear your headspace, but the end product will be a well formatted ebook that won't cause any visual embarrassment to you or the distribution channels.

Go run your own final checks on your Smashwords ebook

At this stage you should again download all the different formats of your ebook from its Smashwords page and check that you like what you see. The checks you are running here are more visual presentation than editing. Does the final product have a look and feel that matches your expectations and does it look comparable with other ebooks you've downloaded? You need to put yourself in the shoes of the purchasing reader.

Channel Manager

You will be informed by email when your ebook has been approved for Premium Catalog. Select your distribution channels, via your Dashboard, in Smashwords Channel Manager and your ebook will be 'shipped' to those retailers on the next scheduled date. It can take two or three weeks before some of the channels feature your ebook in their store. So go to the Sony, Barnes & Noble, Kobo, Apple and Diesel web stores and bookmark them. Ideally register on the sites, if you can (Apple requires that you have an Apple device), and go back periodically to search for your book. If you make any changes to your cover, blurb or price on Smashwords, it will take a similar length of time for those changes to feed through to the channels. Also be aware there are no shared reviews between the product pages (except Kobo links to Goodreads) so your credibility will need to be established on each site.

Coupon Manager

One of the big advantages of Smashwords is you can set up coupons or vouchers that readers can redeem against the purchase price. This gives you the opportunity to offer a discount or, more typically for a new indie author, offer your book for free to selected readers without having to price it at zero for everyone. Situations where this will be useful include member giveaways on LibraryThing, review copies for bloggers and review websites, and freebies for selected friends and family.

Sales & Payment

Your dashboard shows, next to your ebook title, **Books sold** and **Downloads (paid + free samples)**. If you have had any coupons redeemed then they are counted in the copies sold. If you have set price to free and folk have downloaded then those copies are counted in the downloads. Now look in the column on the left of the page.

Total Books sold indicates the number of copies of your ebook that have been purchased direct from Smashwords. This will include voucher purchases, even if they are 100% discount.

Account balance shows the amount of royalty you have earned from Smashwords and distribution channel sales. This is likely to remain at zero for some time for a couple of reasons. First, it's unusual for authors to experience much in the way of direct sales on Smashwords. Second, it takes quite a long time for royalties from distribution channels to feed through the system. (I had assumed that my first novel wasn't selling anything through channels until the figures eventually fed through and I found that Barnes & Noble had shipped 1200 copies!) This delay in sales and royalty figures means that your marketing efforts for those channels won't get any real-time intelligence. For that reason it's a good idea to keep some kind of record of your marketing activities so that you can correlate subsequent sales with relevant marketing efforts e.g. a blog, facebook or twitter push on Nook or Apple ebook formats.

Sales & Payment Report leads to a further page that shows, at the end of that page, the sales reports and payments dates. Click around the page to get familiar with the available information. *Choose a Year* will give a summary breakdown in the left-hand column and a more detailed breakdown at the bottom of the page. Sales reports can also be downloaded. As mentioned above, it may take a few months for distribution channels sales data to feed through.

Other Smashwords features

Smashwords is predominantly a publishing platform, distribution hub and ebook shop. Beyond your dashboard and ebook product pages, most of the other facilities are different listings of the 100,000+ Smashwords published ebooks. There aren't any author or reader chat forums on which to fritter away your valuable writing time. There is a blog that has useful posts and readers can comment. You'll find the blog in the menu options at the bottom of the screen.

Your pricing on the web

Amazon have a minimum ebook price of $0.99. Smashwords have a minimum sales price of $0.99 but you can also give it for free. There is no maximum price but you are unlikely to see much sales volume above $5 unless your book is very unique. Higher priced indie ebooks selling in any volume are typically specialised non-fiction.

There is no obligation to maintain a uniform price for your ebook across different channels but you need to be aware that Amazon reserves the right to adjust the price of your ebook on Amazon if it is offered cheaper elsewhere. Their pricing bots crawl the web and check all kinds of places. Example – I offered 100% Smashwords coupons to bloghop visitors over Christmas 2011. The Amazon bot picked this up and zeroed the price of my first novel for a period of about ten days. It led to nearly 500 copies of my novel being shipped for free by Amazon. The additional readership was welcomed but I had no control over the situation.

Typically, if you offer your Smashwords version cheaper through Barnes & Noble than you do on Amazon, then Amazon are likely to force price parity after a period of a couple of days to a couple of weeks. It can be difficult to control the timing of any further changes and you may have to contact Amazon if they don't change back when you change back your Smashwords price. Remember that the price on Barnes & Noble will lag your Smashwords settings by up to a couple of weeks. In other words, you can play with your prices across Smashwords and Amazon but don't expect to be in control. Ideally, decide upon your pricing strategy and make the changes first on Amazon, then on Smashwords & channels.

Your ebook's reviews on the web

All the ebook stores and reader websites give readers the opportunity to give a rating out of five stars and sometimes write a review for the ebooks they have read. It's worth spending some time understanding how the reviews work because the folk who write your (good) reviews are likely to be your most outspoken and loyal supporters.

With a couple of exceptions (Amazon UK site and Kobo), the reviews are posted individually to each website. A reviewer may well decide to post the same review on several sites, depending upon where they are active, but they will likely have different usernames on each site (because they haven't been thinking brand!) Each site requires the reviewer to be a registered user and some require that the ebook has been purchased on that site.

As a rule of thumb, you can expect one unsolicited review for every 100 or so sales. You will find that some of your most ardent reading fans are reluctant to post reviews. This has all to do with the individual's comfort zone and has to be respected. Other ebook authors are more inclined to write reviews than some readers. We authors are rarely reluctant to shout me, me, me! (I write a lot of reviews, surprise, surprise.) Unless you solicit reviews from your peers or via reading groups, you may well have to wait quite a while for the first unexpected reviews. A new release ebook may take several months to reach 100 sales.

If you do solicit reviews then take care that they are authentic and that the reviewer speaks their mind (within reason) and isn't sycophantic. It's better to have zero reviews than a pile of glowing fake five star praise. If you have engaged in peer groups with your social platform then you will receive occasional unexpected and authentic reviews from other authors.

Whenever you receive a good review (anything from three stars upwards is good) then celebrate! Post it on your facebook wall, tweet it, mention it on your blog. If it makes good copy then add it to your product page on your website / blog and considering including any key phrases in your ebook blurb. I've found that reader reviews have helped me better understand my own books and helped me to articulate the reasons that people enjoy them.

Whenever you receive a low scoring review then let it lie for at least a day and think it over. The reader is quite likely not in your target audience and represents the fringe of your niche or genre. They were attracted to your book by its title, cover, blurb, other reviews or perceived genre but it didn't light their fire. That's okay. You can't please all of the people all of the time; there isn't a universal ebook.

Should you receive an unpleasant review i.e. spiteful, aggressive, insulting, disrespectful or simply irrelevant, then just mentally park it in the trash. Whatever you do, don't respond in any way, except perhaps to flag it to the website where the review was posted. If you feel that you have to mention that unpleasant review anywhere then make sure it's not in any sort of public forum. Whoever wrote that review has things going on in their life that have caused them to vent in the direction of your ebook.

The problem is theirs, not yours. Take the moral high ground. Deep breath, move on.

Here's a brief summary of how reviews work in the main places that your ebook will appear (if you have followed the guidelines in this book).

Amazon - in order for a reader to post a review they must be registered with the Amazon country website and have made a purchase on that country website (the same applies to adding search tags). Kindle customers select their country when they register and they must buy from the site of registration. (If you have a Kindle yourself then note that it is easy to change your kindle country setting by entering a factual postal address in the country of choice.) However, the reviewer doesn't have to have purchased the product that they are reviewing.

It is possible to check out the reviewer's profile on Amazon and read other reviews they've written. Sometimes their profile contains information that leads to a blog or other point of contact, but usually they remain uncontactable and often have an anonymous name.

A review posted on one Amazon site doesn't automatically show up on other country sites. However, reviews posted on a paperback version will also show up under the kindle ebook page on the same country site, and vice versa (this may take some time to appear and contacting via Author central will expedite the connection of kindle and print editions). One feature that Amazon offers is *Was this review helpful to you*. Votes for *Yes* will promote individual reviews to the top of the list on the ebook product page.

Amazon.com usually produces the largest number of reviews, providing that your ebook is selling well through that route. At time of writing, Amazon also has Kindle stores in France, Germany, Italy, Spain and United Kingdom (FR, DE, IT, ES and UK). Any customer who doesn't live in those jurisdictions currently (with a few exceptions based upon common language countries) has to purchase Kindle ebooks via amazon.com e.g. readers in Australia, Canada, Ireland, South America, rest of the world. If the reviewer has purchased the ebook on Amazon then their review will be marked as *Amazon Verified Purchase*.

Amazon.co.uk is the other major English language Amazon Kindle site. Authors often have difficulty in 'crossing the pond' with their ebooks and tend to have more marked sales success either on dot com or UK. Apart from different local tastes in covers and language, the reasons for an ebook's relative success aren't always obvious. The UK site doesn't use the *Amazon Verified Purchase* marker on reviews but it does give a link to any further reviews for that ebook on dot com.

Amazon.de .es .fr and .it sites do not have any review link to dot com. Unless you are able to tap into an ex-patriot or English speaking community in those countries, it's unlikely that you will garner many reviews or sales.

Goodreads tends to have a similar number of reviews per book title as Amazon and sometimes more. Like Amazon, reviews are shared between all editions of the same title, be it paperback, hardback or ebook. Many of the reviews on Goodreads are also posted on Amazon and other ebook stores. Goodreads does sell some ebooks (if the author has enabled that option) but the bulk of readers and reviewers are likely to have purchased their books elsewhere. Like Amazon, a Goodreads purchase isn't mandatory if a reader wants to review a book (Goodreads do offer sale of ebooks but sales volumes are unknown).

Goodreads members can either choose to give a rating out of five stars, leave a written review or both rate and review. Other members can choose to Like the review. Reviewers are far more accessible to the author than on Amazon as clicking on their name will bring you to their member page. However, Goodreads doesn't encourage authors to automatically friend or otherwise communicate with reviewers. This is primarily a readers' community and anything that looks like spamming, auto-following or stalking can result in an author being flagged as a spammer and, after 3 flags, their account may be evaluated for deletion. However, if the reviewer has mentioned something that they wish you to address in the book e.g. typos, then making contact is reasonable.

After you have accumulated a number of reviews you will see that some are from Goodreads friends (some reviewers will have had the self-confidence to offer you their friendship after a favourable review) and some are from the general community (folk who hopefully like your book but they want to keep at arm's length from such a famous author as yourself).

Goodreads also has a function whereby members can add a book to their to-read shelf. This can be the result of recommendations from other members, their having purchased your book but not yet read it or from some interaction with your subtle social network marketing activities. The number of reviews, number of to-read shelvings and overall review score all add into the Goodreads Recommendations engine. Once you get your to-read number in the hundreds you can expect to start showing up in that engine.

LibraryThing operates its reviews process in a very similar way to Goodreads. Members can also Like reviews or flag them as inappropriate or abusive. A good way to build up reviews on LibraryThing is to offer your ebook as a Member Giveaway. Successful recipients are supposed to review your work, if requested. The yield tends to be around 10%.

Smashwords only permits registered members to score and / or review books if they have purchased the book from Smashwords. As most of the books you sell are likely to be via Amazon or Barnes & Noble, it's unlikely that you will gain many reviews on Smashwords. The main exceptions to this will be if you have used Smashwords coupons to give away copies for review, or if you have made the price free and promoted your Smashwords ebook page for downloads.

The same reviews that are posted on Smashwords will often appear reposted by the reviewer on other sites such as Amazon, LibraryThing and Goodreads, particularly if they are gained as the result of copies given away for review.

Barnes & Noble reviewers don't have to purchase a Nook ebook (epub format) to review but they do have to be registered on the site. They can use a pen name for the review or sign it Anonymous. If you are in communication with someone who has posted a review for your ebook elsewhere then it's worth considering asking them to post the review on Barnes & Noble as well, because B&N is likely to be your second largest source of sales.

iTunes has different web stores for different countries. It sells the epub format and readers need to have iTunes installed on their computer or mobile device if they want to purchase via iTunes. The iBookstore is an Apple app that allows Apple device users to browse, purchase and rate ebooks. Ratings on the iTunes country websites are country specific i.e. your ebook may have 7 ratings on the Australian site but none on the Canadian site. Although iTunes is something of a mystery to this dyed-in-the-wool PC user, it's my second best selling ebook channel after Barnes & Noble (have now ordered my iPhone!)

Sony ReaderStore has two sites, one for the US and one for Canada. Users have to register via the Reader Library Software, which restricts the reviewers to Sony Reader owners or users of their Reader Apps. Sony sells ebooks in the lrf file format that you have created through Smashwords.

Diesel reviewers don't have to purchase on Diesel but they are required to register. Diesel offers a financial incentive to reviewers with a few tens of cents reward money for each review you write. There seems to be little crossover between reviews on other sites and the few reviews on Diesel. Diesel sells ebooks in the epub format.

Kobo reviewers can rate a book and must be registered to do so. Kobo displays Goodreads reviews and to place a review on the Kobo site requires the reviewer to do it via Goodreads. The Goodreads reviews are linked to Kobo book pages via the ISBN number on the Goodreads book page. Kobo sells ebooks in epub format.

And finally...

We've reached the end of our journey together with The New Author. If you've stuck with it, you are now an independent ebook author with your finished and polished novel for sale across the globe. You've built a social network platform around your brand, met hundreds of new friends and picked up invaluable advice along the way. Be patient with your ebook sales numbers. Try not to make hasty decisions about your pricing, channels, blurb, cover etc. if the sales volume seems to be taking some time to build. If you suspect that something isn't right with your product presentation and positioning then consult your peers and take seriously the feedback from those whose opinion you have grown to respect.

The most important thing of all is to keep writing. Work at your social network, leverage all the components to build your brand and promote your ebook in ways that are palatable to your target market, but keep on writing. Unlike print books, your ebook doesn't have a finite shelf life. Your novel is a good book, it will establish a reader base and grow in popularity with your target group of readers. But it's going to be lonely on that virtual shelf all by itself. You need to write another book, and another. The independent authors that achieve strong and steady success, be it in terms of income and / or readership, are those with a backlist of titles. In a couple of years from now that could be you.

I wrote The New Author with the specific intention of helping folk to deal with just three areas that can be a challenge: writing your novel, building a social media platform, and publishing an independent ebook. There are two other topics that I'm going to touch on briefly before we draw things to a close with some reading recommendations.

Self-publishing in print

The epublishing revolution means that an ever-increasing number of readers are turning to ebooks. News agencies continuously quote figures from different sources that show ebook sales overtaking print book sales in various markets. However, that means that around half of the reading public still buy print. To only publish as an ebook is to miss that sector of the market. Many friends, colleagues and associates have told me they would love to buy my novels if only they were available in print.

Having published your novel as an ebook, you know that it isn't vanity publishing. For some people it may be, but not for you. You have slaved over your manuscript, edited it, had it beta-read, copy-edited, etc. The packaging, your cover and blurb, are polished and you have a carefully thought out brand, enhanced by a social network platform. You are serious about this independent epublishing business. But to put your book out as a paperback, wouldn't that be vanity publishing? Not necessarily.

In the way that ebooks have blurred the margins of mainstream and vanity publishing, so print-on-demand (POD) technology is doing the same with the paperback market. POD companies can print a single, high quality paperback copy of your book and ship it to the purchaser within hours of an order being placed. No stock has to be held anywhere. The costs are low enough that end selling prices remain competitive and the author earns a better cut than would be provided by mainstream publishing. It's definitely something to consider, although you may wish to build your readership and brand momentum before you dive in. I'll return to POD for independent authors at a later date.

Marketing an ebook

I haven't taken a prescriptive approach to ebook marketing in The New Author. There are titles available that do so, and I mention a few of them in the recommended reading section that's coming up soon. But throughout these pages you will have sensed the implicit marketing strategy that I believe works with ebooks. Traditional in-your-face product marketing doesn't work for ebooks. What does work is recommendation by people who have read and enjoyed your book. This may be by word of mouth, on reader websites or through reviews posted on websites. It's a snowball that you have to start rolling down the mountain.

When highly successful independent ebook authors are asked to describe how they achieved their sales, brand strength and market exposure, they can rarely put their finger on the critical success factors. It sometimes comes over as enigmatic, that they don't want to divulge their secrets in case everybody else copies the method and dilutes their success. Whereas the truth likely is they really don't know what the catalyst was. (An exception would be any author with a substantial backlist of books and a sizeable email list.)

The key to this conundrum is exposure. A new ebook launched by a major publisher can reach the top hundred on Amazon, Barnes & Noble etc without any reviews, tags, twitter or blog posts. The publisher and ebook seller arrange for promotion of the new release to a profiled section of an enormous customer base. The ebook gets immediate exposure to a buying public, hungry for something new and exciting. As an independent author, your objective is to somehow emulate that, to get exposure for your ebook.

You might achieve exposure in any number of ways. Perhaps you have or can develop a talent for rhetoric and write amazing blog posts that go viral. You may become a twitter grand master and create irresistible hooks within 140 characters. Maybe you are or will be the doyenne of a huge online community that will follow your Pied Piper tracks to Amazon and hit that *Buy now* button. You might work quietly and consistently at all the components of your brand network and build a momentum that will propel your ebook gradually into the bright light. Or perhaps you'll just get lucky.

As an end note, *Vignette 3 – Under the influence* shows some of the buttons that marketeers aim to push when trying to influence a purchaser. Read it and see how it makes you feel. The epublishing world contains a full spectrum of marketing approaches, from fully in-your-face to subliminal. You will find the approach that you're comfortable with and, sooner or later, it's going to work for you.

~~~

Vignette 3 - Under the influence - social networks

This item was originally posted July 31st 2011 on the Ruby Barnes blog and provides some uncomfortable insights into marketing strategies.

I'm going to engage in a little bit of harmless ebook marketing, by way of illustration, so please bear with me. The following may read crass to you, but it's just for purpose of illustration.

Every week I throw out food that is spoilt, has passed its sell-buy date or just isn't wanted anymore. I imagine many of you do too. Dollars, Euros, pounds worth of food thrown away, wasted. What do you get for that wasted money? Nothing. In contrast, my quirky crime novel Peril is yours for just $2.99. For $2.99 you get a 4 / 5 star rated ebook of 90,000 words. Why am I almost giving it away, this full-length novel? Because I want people to read it. [1]

It gets better. During summer 2011 Peril is available for free. Absolutely free. No strings. If you would like to leave a review on Amazon, Smashwords, Goodreads or anywhere then that's appreciated, but it's your decision. If you like it, you might tell your friends and colleagues, and you might like the upcoming novel The Baptist, by the same author. [2]

A quick word to the thousands of people who already took the plunge and bought Peril or downloaded it free from Smashwords since it was launched in March 2011 - The Baptist will be available in time for Christmas 2011. You can give it as a present to yourselves, family and friends. [3]

Many people have left their honest opinion of Peril in the ether of Amazon, Goodreads, Smashwords and various other websites. People enjoy this book. There have been almost no bad reviews. If you haven't read it already then these people say you're in for a treat! [4]

Who am I to thrust my book upon you? I'm just an independent, self-kindled author, writing in memory of my grandfather Robert Barnes who slaved in the shipyards of Glasgow, building great ships during a bygone, golden era. These days I live in beautiful Ireland, the Emerald Isle. A land of tranquillity to which so many people can trace their roots. My only claim on this proud and ancient Ireland is that some of my ancestors originated here and I am truly thankful to God and society for providing me with an occupation, three beautiful children and a supportive and understanding wife. [5]

It humbles me that Peril is endorsed by authors of note in several genres on five continents. In all honesty and modesty I never expected that my work would sit before them and be enjoyed. [6]

Just another mention that Peril is free on Smashwords for summer 2011, but only a further fifty copies are available under this offer. In autumn Peril's price tag will revert to $7.99 or thereabouts. At year end it will likely be permanently withdrawn, left in ownership of those select readers that have ventured to add a little Peril to their lives. [7]

Disclaimer: the above is an exercise!

Is it overwhelming? Nauseating, repulsive? In parts perhaps. But there is nothing in there, nothing, that isn't present in modern-day marketing.

One of my favourite business books is Robert Cialdini's 'Influence - the Psychology of Persuasion'. There are many books on how to apply influence but this book is fun to read, thanks to the many anecdotes and case studies. It'll leave the hairs standing up on your neck as you fully realise just how manipulative the marketing process can be. Cialdini identifies a number of principles - weapons of influence - that you will recognise. The little skit above attempts to use these in the context of promoting an ebook, but I'm going to expand upon seven identified weapons of influence in the context of social network marketing as an author (blog, twitter, facebook etc.)

The bracketed numbers in the above example are referenced to each weapon of influence below.

[1] Perceptual contrast

The idea here is to make the target (yes, target!) feel that their purchase isn't of financial consequence but, nevertheless, is of great value, a no-brainer. This can be done with a price reduction, if credible. It can also be done by comparison with traditional printed books. Why pay $14.99 for a paperback that will fall to pieces when you drop it in the bath (okay, bad example, don't drop your e-reader or laptop in the bath, shows what an intrinsically bad marketeer I am!) Let's try this: the facilities available for ebooks - speech to text, bookmarking, updates etc. - far exceed paper books and yet you can get your ebook for somewhere between 99c and $5. What are you waiting for?

[2] Reciprocation

This is where you make the customer feel obligated by giving them something extra. In real life the dinner invitation is a good example. Only sociopaths don't feel the need to reciprocate a pleasant dinner invitation. In fact, the rule of reciprocation is so strong that it can lead to a lifetime pattern of tit-for-tat dinners with people who you eventually come to classify as friends.

In the ebook social network marketing context, a free giveaway is often used but care has to be taken not to devalue the product. Other manifestations are mutual reviews between authors and requests for beta readers.

If you are asked and agree to take a book for review, and then fail to deliver that review, it will burn a hole in your conscience. If you write a review it is likely to be favourable. Another reciprocation favourite is the retweeting of twitter influencers. They'll be beholden to you and that credit can be cashed in whenever you want. That's the pleasure of giving!

[3] Commitment and consistency

Once the target reader has made their purchase of your ebook, or has taken up the free 'no strings attached' offer, they are on a track that will take a special effort on their part to leave. Build up that readership by any of the methods mentioned here and that same readership will substantially follow your next release (at full price) and review it favourably. Of course, a fanbase is built upon satisfied customers but what you are looking to do is built brand loyalty. The product has to be reasonably good and well packaged, but needn't be exceptional.

[4] Social proof

I'm going to refer to Cialdini's example of canned laughter. With your influence radar switched on, canned laughter is a ridiculously artificial contruct. But you'll likely find that most of the successful TV sitcoms are continuously swaddled in the stuff. *Friends*, for example. Compare that with the true life audience mirth of *Fawlty Towers* or *Monty Python* (who? okay, you're not all as ancient as me) or live comedy.

If you have the impression that the populace approves the product then you, if you want to conform to the image of a discerning consumer, are likely to follow suit. Nine out of ten owners (who expressed a preference) said their cats preferred it, sort of thing. In the case of ebooks, viral marketing can build a self-perpetuating myth. Program your tweetdeck or other tool with repetitive messages to tell the world that the world is approving your product.

[5] Liking

People buy things from people who they like. The important thing here is to understand the target demographic. A select number of people might like an author who is ironic. Other readers will like an underdog. Some will be looking for admirable virtues. A bio that makes potential readers like the author can make the difference between carry-on-browsing and click-to-purchase.

[6] Authority

Endorsement carries great weight. I'll come clean and say that section 6 of the skit above is Peril's weakest link. If I could evidence written endorsements from successful authors in different geographic markets - quirky, award winning, best selling US and UK authors - then my ebook would ride upon their wave. Hey, wait. I have an endorsement for *The New Author*!

[7] Scarcity

People like to know that what they purchase has an even greater value due to constricted availability. People pay good money for limited edition prints and first edition hardback books. For ebooks it's more of a challenge but might include special versions with artwork or personal messages and electronically signed copies.

Next time you're on the receiving end of social network marketing, stop for a second and consider whether you are being manipulated by weapons of influence. We've all been the targets of influence strategies throughout our lives.

Recognising and differentiating a genuine offer from an influence strategy is only the first step. Resisting influence tactics is very difficult. The rule of reciprocation, for example, will make you feel guilty if you don't respond. Understanding the sincerity of the sentiment can help you to override intuitive reaction. A skilful marketeer can dress weapons of influence so they appear genuine.

For those who are or would be influential marketeers, can you build your marketing plan - based upon the principles of persuasion and maintain your integrity? I'm not sure that I can. I'm just not clever enough.

~~~

RUBY BARNES

I hope you have enjoyed The New Author. Please consider writing a review of this book on Goodreads, LibraryThing, Amazon, Barnes & Noble and other websites. All feedback is highly welcomed.

If you have any suggestions or comments then please mail me ruby.barnes@marblecitypublishing.com or surf over to my blog and contact me there at http://rubybarnes.blogspot.com.

The following *Ruby's Top Ten Tips for Ebook Publishing* gives a summary of everything we have covered in this book. You should now feel ready and able to join the epublishing revolution. I wish you all the very best with your ebook sales.

~~~

RUBY BARNES

Ruby's Top Ten Tips
for Ebook Publishing

1. You're going to need a good book, one you believe in, one that has your author's voice. That unique voice communicates your individual talent as a writer.

2. Test your book on honest people before you consider releasing it. Make it the absolute best you can. Don't regret, be proud.

3. Ready to publish? Forget about it until you've considered the next two marketing steps of platform and brand. You can ignore them and still be successful. That will make you into a folklore hero whose name is on everybody's lips, but they're few and far between (and I'm not one of them).

4. You need a social networking platform. Ebook readers are internet users. That's where you need to focus (and make sure you start that ball rolling before launching your ebook).

5. Brand is to an author what location is to real estate. Make your name your brand. Everything you do needs to enhance that brand. Exert caution at this point because, if you do it wrong, retracing your steps is difficult.

6. Now let's publish. A cover, title and description that tells a potential reader that your novel is worth reading. A digital manuscript that won't cause that reader to trip over systemic errors in prose, grammar or format. If you baulk at any of this then pay someone who can do the uncomfortable parts for you (it can be less expensive than you might think). And keep backups and version control for everything that you write.

7. Aim to build a readership that will provide reviews, recommendations and support. Don't be precious about initial pricing.

8. Leverage your social networking platform to gradually increase exposure of your book. Use subliminal marketing and influence strategies when you enter into the mêlée of the marketplace.

9. Build your brand team. Remember at every step that each virtual friend, follower and reader is your team. Never alienate, even when in receipt of negativity. Radiate positivity and calm confidence. People don't just read your ebook, they also digest your blog posts, forum comments, tweets, facebook updates, everything that you write on the internet. Those readers read, enjoy and recommend. Word of mouth sells ebooks. This is the key.

10. Are you writing the next book? Never stop writing creatively. Always have a project in the first draft or edit stages. Blogging, tweeting, chatting and whatever is new, all good but you are an author and you must write. Allocate time for making friends and marketing. Ring-fence time for creative writing. Do both, in parallel, with an element of self-discipline. A satisfied reader asks for more. The reader market is effectively infinite and so is their appetite for good books.

Recommended reading

The following print and ebooks have been found very useful by a wide number of authors. Style of delivery varies widely but they're all good. When considering these books, I suggest you browse before purchase to ensure that they have the type of content you are looking for.

Mainstream authors

Becoming a Writer by Dorothea Brande

Mystery and Manners by Flannery O'Connor

On Becoming a Novelist by John Gardner

The Seven Basic Plots by Christopher Booker

Writing Alone and with Others by Pat Schneider

Negotiating with the Dead - by Margaret Atwood - A writer on writing

The Practice of Writing by David Lodge

The Artist's Way by Julia Cameron - A course in discovering and recovering your creative self

Bird By Bird - Some Instructions on Writing and Life by Anne Lamott

A Whore's Profession by David Mamet

The First Five Pages - A Writer's Guide to Staying Out of the Rejection Pile by Noah Lukeman

Self-Editing for Fiction Writers by Renni Browne and Dave King

Eats, Shoots and Leaves by Lynne Truss

Guide to Punctuation by R.I. Trask

On Writing by Stephen King

How NOT to Write a Novel: 200 Mistakes to avoid at All Costs if You Ever Want to Get Published by Mittelmark and Newman – extremely funny if you like their sense of humour, full of hilarious examples of how not to do it!

Influence - the Psychology of Persuasion by Robert Cialdini - more or less any successful marketing approach leverages these principles

Abnormal Psychology by David S Holmes - because it's good to have your serial killers and psychopathic characters clinically correct

Independent Authors

Nail Your Novel – Why Writers Abandon Books and How You Can Draft, Fix and Finish With Confidence by Roz Morris – a method approach to novel writing

How I Sold 1 Million eBooks in 5 Months! by John Locke – an account of the successes and failures of different ebook marketing methods by a master of rhetoric

Smashwords Style Guide by Mark Croker – the definitive formatting guide for Smashwords by the founder of the company

Smashwords Book Marketing Guide by Mark Croker – how best to market an ebook via Smashwords

Format Your eBook for Kindle in One Hour - A Step-by-Step Guide by Derek J. Canyon – a method approach to kindle formatting that uses a standard html template

We Are Not Alone: The Writer's Guide to Social Media by Kristen Lamb – a very energizing approach to social media marketing for writers

RUBY BARNES

Index

D

E

F

G

H

I

K

L

M

N

O

P

R

S

T

W

Contact Ruby Barnes

Connect with me online:

Email: ruby.barnes@marblecitypublishing.com

My Blog: http://rubybarnes.blogspot.com

Twitter: http://twitter.com/Ruby_Barnes

Facebook page: Ruby Barnes

Facebook person: RubyBarnesBooks

I've pedalled the pushbike of life through the Shires' rolling hills, along the folded rocks of Scotland's lochs and out west to the fractured reaches of North Wales. Love found me in the MacGillycuddy's Reeks of Ireland. The Swiss Alps cured me of obsessive compulsion and yielded progeny.

Misfits, rogues and psychopaths take form in Peril, The Baptist and other works. Their voices, they speak to me. I plead with them, but the demons are real. I've carried them on my back across Scandinavia, through the Mid-West, Eastern Seaboard and Deep South of the USA and to the borders of Argentina, Brazil and Paraguay. We teetered together on the brink of the Iguassu Falls and came back.

My writing is dedicated to the memory of my late grandfather Robert 'Ruby' Barnes.

Other books by Ruby Barnes

If you've enjoyed The New Author then try **Peril**, the first novel from Ruby Barnes.

A contemporary crime thriller set in Dublin, Ireland.

Some readers' thoughts:

Full of sharp wit and realistic characters, this book does exactly what it sets out to do - take readers on an adventure and leave them wondering what could possibly happen next.

Ruby Barnes has taken a character's life and spins a web that keeps you reading until the very end.

Ger is an anti-hero, the lad all the lads want to be, the guy all the girls love to hate but just can't bring themselves to. Scrape after scrape, he trundles through life with all the awareness of a rock, and yet you just can't help rooting for him...

Like nothing I've ever read before. The story is well written with a fast pace, intriguing plot twists and a good balance of dark humour and human drama.

You won't want to put it down... it twists and turns like a twisty turny thing.

A fantastic read, one of those rare books that keeps you guessing.

Gerard Mayes is in a bind. He's committed most of the seven deadly sins and is trying to avoid paying the price.

'I balance on the precipice of life. Friends and family have turned their backs on me and walked into the shadowland. Police and thieves are shouting Jump, Ger. Do it.'

Ladies, don't let your man read this book. You don't want him getting ideas on how to misbehave.

Fellas, keep your copy of Peril well hidden.